WHAT IS THE BOOK OF JOB?

What Is the Book of

JOB?

Michael Whitworth

ISBN 978-1-971767-24-6

Published by Start2Finish
Bend, Oregon 97702
start2finish.org

Printed in the United States of America
30 29 28 27 26   1 2 3 4 5

CONTENTS

WHY WASN'T I STILLBORN?

From cursing his birthday, Job shifts to a painful question: Why didn't I just die at birth? "Why did I not die when I came out of the womb? Why were there knees to receive me and breasts to nurse me? If I had died then, I would be at rest now."

He imagines what it would have been like to go straight from the womb to the grave. And here's the part that catches you off guard: he describes death as something beautiful. Restful. Peaceful. In death, he says, he would be lying down in quiet. He would be sleeping. He would be alongside kings and rulers who built great things during their lives but who are now at rest, finished with their work.

He goes even further. In death, the wicked stop causing trouble. Prisoners no longer hear the voice of the slave driver. The small and the great are there together, and the slave is finally free from his master. Death, in Job's eyes, is not a horror—it's a release. It's the one place where the pain stops and nobody can hurt you anymore.

For a man who believes in God, these are startling words. Job isn't describing heaven; the ancient Israelites didn't have a fully developed idea of an afterlife the way we do. He's describing the grave as simple, silent rest. And in his current state of agony, that sounds better than anything life has to offer.

WHY DOES GOD KEEP THE MISERABLE ALIVE?

The final section of Job's speech is the sharpest. He stops talking about himself specifically and asks a broader question: Why does God give life to people who don't want it?

"Why is light given to those in misery, and life to the bitter in soul, who long for death but it doesn't come, who search for it more than for buried treasure, who would celebrate if they could find the grave?"

That image—of people digging for death the way treasure hunters dig for gold—is one of the most haunting pictures in the entire Bible. Job is saying that for some people, dying would feel like striking it rich. That's how unbearable their existence has become.

Then he makes it personal again: "Why is life given to a man whose way is hidden, whom God has fenced in?"

That last phrase is a painful echo of something said earlier in the book. Back in chapter 1, the accuser told God that the reason Job was so faithful was because God had put a protective "hedge" around him, a fence that kept all harm away. Now Job uses the same word, but the meaning has flipped completely. The fence that once protected him now feels like a prison. God isn't keeping danger out. God is keeping Job *in*, trapped in his suffering with no way of escape.

Job finishes with raw, unfiltered honesty: "I have no ease. I have no quiet. I have no rest. Only turmoil."

That's it. That's where the speech ends. No resolution. No prayer. No turning to God in hope. Just a man at the bottom of the deepest pit he's ever been in, crying out into the dark.

DID JOB SIN?

Here's the question you're probably asking: Did Job go too far?

Think about it. He cursed the day God gave him life. He wished he had never been born. He described God as someone who traps miserable people in their suffering. He didn't pray. He didn't praise. He didn't turn toward God at all. He spoke into the air, to no one in particular.

And yet the text never says Job sinned. Not here. Not in this speech.

That matters enormously. Because it tells us something about God that we desperately need to hear: God can handle your honesty. He is not threatened by your pain. He doesn't require you to paste on a brave face and pretend everything is fine when your world is falling apart.

Job didn't curse God. That's the line the accuser predicted he would cross, and he didn't cross it. But he came right up to the edge. He poured out the darkest, rawest, most desperate words a human being can speak—and God let him. There was no lightning bolt. No rebuke from heaven. No voice from the clouds saying, "How dare you."

Just silence. And three friends sitting in the ashes, stunned by what they'd just heard.

WHAT THIS MEANS FOR US

First, grief doesn't follow a schedule. Job held it together for seven days and then fell apart. That's how grief works. You might be fine on the day of the funeral and collapse three weeks later in a grocery store. There's no "right" timeline for pain, and there's nothing wrong with you if your worst moment comes long after the crisis itself.

Second, honest pain is not the same as lost faith. Job's words in chapter 3 are some of the darkest in the Bible, but the narrator never calls them sin. You can be devastated, furious, confused, and heartbroken—and still belong to God. Faith isn't the absence of anguish. It's what keeps you from walking away entirely, even when you can't see any reason to stay.

Third, wishing the pain would end is not the same as giving up on God. Job wanted to die, but he never considered taking his own life. Even in his deepest agony, he recognized that his life was not his to throw away. It was a gift, even if it felt like a cruel one. If you ever find yourself in a place so dark that you wish you could disappear, please know that those feelings are real and they matter, but they are not the final word. Talk to someone you trust. You are not alone, and your story is not over.

Fourth, sometimes the most spiritual thing you can do is stop performing and start telling the truth. Job didn't offer a polished prayer. He didn't recite a creed. He screamed into the void. And somehow, that raw honesty was more real—more *human*—than a thousand carefully worded devotionals. God would rather hear your real voice, even if it's shaking, than a rehearsed one that doesn't mean anything.

TALKING POINTS

1. **Job went from worshiping God after losing everything (chapter 1) to cursing the day he was born (chapter 3).** How do you explain the change? Does this mean his faith in chapter 1 wasn't real?

2. **Job described death as a place of rest and peace.** Why do you think suffering made the grave sound so appealing to him? How does believing in an afterlife change the way we think about pain?

3. Job used the image of God "fencing him in," the same word the accuser used for God's protective hedge. What does it tell us about suffering that the same God who protects us can sometimes feel like the one trapping us?

4. The text never says Job sinned in this speech. Do you think there's a difference between being angry at your situation and being angry at God? Where is the line between honest grief and losing faith?

5. Job's three friends had been sitting in silence for seven days when this speech erupted. If you were one of Job's three friends and you'd just heard this speech after seven days of silence, what would you be feeling? What would you want to say, and should you say it?

The silence is shattered. Job has spoken, and his words hang in the air like smoke. His friends have just heard a man they admired, a man they came to comfort, sound like someone who has lost all hope. They can't just sit there anymore. Somebody has to respond.

Turn the page.

3

FRIENDS WHO MAKE IT WORSE

Remember Anxiety from *Inside Out 2*? Riley is thirteen, starting high school hockey camp, desperate to fit in with the older girls. And then Anxiety shows up inside her head: a jittery, orange, well-meaning emotion who genuinely believes she's helping. Anxiety doesn't want to hurt Riley. She wants to protect her. She's convinced that if Riley doesn't plan for every possible disaster, everything will fall apart. So Anxiety takes over headquarters, shoves Joy and the other emotions aside, and starts running the show.

The results are catastrophic. Riley starts lying. She abandons her real friends. She turns herself inside out trying to be someone she's not. Her sense of self literally gets dismantled and rebuilt into something fragile and fake. And the whole time, Anxiety keeps insisting she's doing the right thing. She has a theory about what Riley needs, she's absolutely sure she's right, and the more things go wrong, the harder she pushes.

That's what happens when someone who cares about you is operating from the wrong diagnosis. They can be sincere. They can be smart. They can genuinely love you. But if their understanding of the problem is wrong, every solution they offer will only make things worse.

Job is about to find that out. The silence is over. His three friends are about to open their mouths. And for the next eleven chapters, they are going to be the most well-meaning, theologically confident, devastatingly unhelpful counselors in the history of the world.

MEET THE FRIENDS

Before we walk through what they say, you need to understand the idea that drives all three of them. It's called the retribution principle, and it goes like this: God rewards the righteous and punishes the wicked. Good people prosper. Bad people suffer. If something wonderful happens to you, it's because you're living right. If something terrible happens to you, it's because you've done something wrong.

This idea wasn't invented by Job's friends. It runs through a lot of the Old Testament. The book of Proverbs is full of it. And in a general sense, it's not entirely wrong. There *is* a connection between how you live and how your life tends to go. Honest people tend to earn trust. Lazy people tend to struggle. Wisdom tends to lead to better outcomes than foolishness.

The problem is what happens when you turn a general tendency into an absolute rule. When you take "the righteous usually prosper" and harden it into "anyone who suffers must have sinned," you've built a system that has no room for people like Job. And that's exactly what the friends do. They take a true-ish idea and wield it like a hammer, and the person under the hammer is their closest friend.

Each of the three friends approaches the problem from a slightly different angle, but they all arrive at the same conclusion: Job must have done something wrong.

ELIPHAZ: THE GENTLE OPENER

Eliphaz speaks first, probably because he's the oldest. And to his credit, he starts carefully. He acknowledges that Job used to be the one giving comfort to others—strengthening weak hands, lifting up people who were stumbling. He reminds Job of his own faith. Then he asks a question that sounds reasonable on the surface: "Think about it: who that was innocent ever perished? Where were the upright ever destroyed?"

It sounds almost kind. Eliphaz is saying, "Job, you're a good man. Good men don't stay down. This will pass."

But listen to what's underneath: if the innocent never perish, and Job is perishing, then maybe Job isn't as innocent as he thinks. Eliphaz doesn't say that outright—not yet. But the logic is there, ticking like a bomb.

He backs up his case with a spooky nighttime vision. A spirit whispered a message to him in the dark: "Can a mortal be righteous before God? Can a man be pure before his Maker?" Even the angels aren't fully trustworthy, Eliphaz says. How much less a human being, fragile as a moth, made of dust and clay? His point is that no one is truly blameless in God's eyes, which conveniently explains Job's suffering without Eliphaz needing to name a specific sin.

Then he delivers his prescription: if it were me, I'd turn to God. I'd lay my case before him. God wounds, but he also binds up. God is disciplining you, Job. Don't reject it. Accept the correction, and everything will be restored.

It sounds wise. It sounds helpful. And it's almost entirely wrong because Eliphaz is treating a formula like a fact. He's so certain the universe runs on a simple reward-and-punishment system that he can't even imagine a scenario where a righteous man suffers for no reason at all. But that's exactly the scenario the reader already knows about from chapters 1–2.

JOB FIRES BACK

Job's response is raw. He doesn't politely disagree. He erupts.

First, he defends the intensity of his pain. If you could weigh my anguish, he says, it would be heavier than the sand of the seas. That's why my words have been wild. He's saying: *You don't understand what this feels like. Don't lecture me about composure when you have no idea what I'm carrying.*

Then he turns on his friends with one of the most cutting metaphors in the Bible. He compares them to a desert stream, a wadi that's full and rushing during the rainy season but completely dry when you actually need water. Caravans count on that stream. They travel across the desert expecting to find it. But when they arrive, the riverbed is empty, and they die of thirst. That's what you are to me, Job says. I needed you, and you have nothing.

He doesn't ask them for money. He doesn't ask them to fight his battles. All he asks is: show me where I'm wrong. If I've sinned, point to it. Give me evidence. But they can't. They have a theory, not a case.

And then Job does something that would have made his

friends' blood run cold. He turns away from them and starts talking to God directly—not in worship, but in accusation. Am I the sea or some kind of monster that you need to keep me under guard? Why have you made me your target? Why don't you just forgive whatever I've done and leave me alone? His words drip with bitterness. The man who once worshiped God after losing everything is now demanding that God explain himself.

BILDAD: BLUNTER AND COLDER

Bildad is less diplomatic than Eliphaz. He essentially tells Job to stop talking. "How long will you go on like this? Your words are nothing but wind."

Then he says something breathtakingly cruel: "If your children sinned against God, he gave them over to their sin." Read that again. Bildad is suggesting that Job's ten children—the children Job grieved and buried—*got what they deserved*. He doesn't say it with malice. He says it as though he's stating an obvious fact. That's how deeply the retribution principle has shaped his thinking. Suffering equals punishment. Even the death of children must have a cause.

His advice? Seek God. Be pure. If you're truly blameless, God will restore you. Your beginning may have been small, but your future will be great.

It's a promise built on a lie. Bildad has no idea whether God will restore Job. He's just assuming the formula works, that if Job pushes the right buttons, the machine will produce the right result.

JOB'S RESPONSE: THE IMPOSSIBLE COURTROOM

Job doesn't argue with Bildad's theology directly. Instead, he asks a question that cuts deeper: "How can a mortal be righteous before God?" Even if I wanted to make my case, how could I? God is so powerful that mountains don't even know when he moves them. He shakes the earth. He commands the sun not to rise. He does things so great and so incomprehensible that no one can understand them.

This sounds like praise, but it's actually a complaint. Job is saying that God is so overwhelming that there's no way to get a fair hearing. If I summoned God to court, he wouldn't show up. If he did show up, he'd crush me with a storm. Even if I were completely innocent, my own mouth would condemn me under the sheer weight of his presence.

And then Job says something that will echo through the rest of the book: "If only there were someone to mediate between us, someone who could lay a hand on both of us—on God and on me." He wants a referee. An umpire. Someone who can stand between him and God and make sure the proceedings are fair. It's a longing that won't go away, and it will surface again and again in the chapters to come.

ZOPHAR: THE HARSHEST YET

Zophar has had enough. He's the youngest and the least patient, and he doesn't bother with pleasantries. He accuses Job of being a babbling fool. He tells Job that God is actually letting him off easy, that if God really gave Job what he deserved, it would be far worse. "Know this," Zophar says. "God has even forgotten some of your sin."

It's the cruelest thing anyone has said so far. Not only is Job guilty, but he's *more* guilty than his suffering even reflects. God, in Zophar's view, is actually being merciful by not punishing Job enough.

JOB'S FINAL WORD: HOPE THAT FLICKERS AND DIES

Job's response to Zophar is the longest and most powerful speech of the first cycle. He begins with bitter sarcasm: "No doubt you are the people, and wisdom will die with you!" He's saying, "Oh, of course—you three have all the answers. What would the world do without your brilliance?"

Then he makes a devastating argument. He points to the real world and says: look around. The tents of robbers are secure. People who provoke God live in safety. Ask the animals, ask the birds, ask the fish. They all know that God's hand controls everything. And what does that hand do? It tears down what cannot be rebuilt. It strips wisdom from leaders. It makes judges into fools. It leads nations to greatness and then destroys them.

Job isn't denying God's power. He's terrified of it. Because if God is this powerful and this unpredictable, then no formula can protect you. The retribution principle crumbles. You can do everything right and still be crushed.

He turns to his friends one last time and calls them "worthless physicians," doctors who diagnose an illness they don't understand and prescribe medicine that doesn't work. "Your best wisdom," he tells them, "would be silence."

And then, in one of the most haunting passages in the Old Testament, Job looks at a tree. A tree that's been cut down can sprout again. If its roots catch water, it will send up new shoots. But a man? A man dies and is laid low. He breathes his last and is gone. "If a man dies, will he live again?"

For one brief, shimmering moment, Job lets himself imagine something extraordinary—what if God hid him in the grave until his anger passed, and then *remembered* him? What if there was an appointed time when God would call, and Job would answer, and the whole terrible misunderstanding would be resolved?

But the hope collapses almost as soon as it appears. Mountains erode. Water wears away stone. And God destroys the hope of mortals in the same relentless way. The vision dies. Job is left with nothing but the pain of his own body and grief for his own soul.

The first round is over. Nobody won.

WHAT THIS MEANS FOR US

First, a wrong diagnosis leads to a wrong prescription. The friends weren't stupid. They were working from a theology that had real roots in Scripture. But they applied it mechanically, without mercy, and without any willingness to let their friend's actual experience challenge their theory. When someone is hurting, the worst thing you can do is force their pain into a box that doesn't fit.

Second, sometimes the most honest thing you can say is "I don't know." Not one of Job's friends ever says those three words. They always have an answer. They always have a theory. And their certainty does more damage than their theology. The bravest, most faithful response to someone else's suffering is often just admitting that you don't understand it either.

Third, wanting answers from God is not the same as rejecting God. Job is furious. He's accusing. He's demanding a hearing. But he's still talking *to* God, or at least *about* God. He hasn't walked away. The fact that he wants a mediator, someone to stand between him and God, shows that he still believes a relationship with God is worth fighting for, even when that relationship feels like a war.

Fourth, the desire for justice is built into us by God himself. Job's longing for a fair hearing isn't arrogance. It's the cry of a creature made in God's image who knows, deep in his bones, that things are not the way they're supposed to be. That cry doesn't go unanswered forever, but the answer won't come in the way Job expects.

TALKING POINTS

1. **Eliphaz told Job that innocent people don't perish.** Is that true? Can you think of examples, from the Bible or from life, where innocent people suffered? Why do you think people find it so comforting to believe that suffering always has a reason?

2. **Job compared his friends to a dry riverbed—full when you don't need them, empty when you do.** Have you ever felt that way about someone? What makes the difference between a friend who helps in hard times and one who doesn't?

3. **Bildad suggested that Job's children died because of their own sin.** Why is that such a harmful thing to say? What does it reveal about how the retribution principle can go wrong?

4. **Job longed for a mediator: someone to stand between him and God.** As a Christian, who do you think fills that

role? How does knowing about Jesus change the way you read Job's wish?

5. **Job imagined a tree sprouting again after being cut down, and then asked, "If a man dies, will he live again?"** Why do you think he couldn't hold on to that hope? How does the resurrection of Jesus speak into Job's question?

The friends have made their case. Job has pushed back hard. But nobody is backing down. The arguments are about to get sharper, the accusations more personal, and the stakes even higher. Round two is coming.

Turn the page.

4

WHEN THE ARGUMENT GETS UGLY

There's a scene in *Anne of Green Gables* that sticks with you long after you've read it. Marilla Cuthbert can't find her precious amethyst brooch—a small piece of jewelry with enormous sentimental value—and she becomes convinced that Anne stole it. Anne insists she didn't. She says it over and over. But Marilla won't budge. The evidence, in Marilla's mind, is clear: Anne was the last person to handle the brooch, Anne has a wild imagination and a history of getting into trouble, and therefore Anne must be the thief.

What makes the scene so painful is that Marilla isn't a villain. She's a decent, moral woman who genuinely cares about Anne. But she's made up her mind, and once she has, nothing Anne says can change it. Every denial just makes her look more guilty. Every protest is treated as further proof that she's lying. Anne is caught in a system where her innocence actually works against her because in Marilla's framework, only a guilty person would keep insisting she's innocent.

Eventually, Anne fabricates a confession just to end the argument and get permission to go to the picnic. She tells

Marilla exactly what Marilla wants to hear: a detailed story about taking the brooch, losing it, the whole thing. Marilla believes every word and punishes her. It's only later that the brooch turns up exactly where Marilla left it, and the whole accusation collapses.

The second cycle of speeches in Job feels a lot like that scene, except Anne's ordeal lasted a few days. Job's lasts for months. His friends are absolutely certain they know what's wrong. They've made their diagnosis, and they're not interested in evidence. And the harder Job pushes back, the angrier they get.

Welcome to round two.

THE GLOVES COME OFF

The first round of speeches had at least a veneer of gentleness. Eliphaz started with a compliment. Bildad appealed to tradition. Even Zophar, the harshest of the three, was trying to nudge Job toward repentance. They were wrong, but they were at least pretending to be helpful.

Round two drops the pretense.

In the first cycle, the friends gave advice. In the second cycle, they paint pictures—long, vivid, terrifying portraits of what happens to wicked people. And every single portrait is aimed at Job.

The shift is dramatic. In round one, the friends spent most of their time urging Job to turn back to God. In round two, they spend almost all their time describing the horrifying fate of the wicked. They talk about the wicked man writhing in pain, hearing terrifying sounds, wandering in darkness. They describe his wealth evaporating, his children begging, his body consumed by disease. They describe him being vomited out of his prosperity, struck through with arrows, swallowed by darkness.

They never say "Job, this is you." They don't have to. Every image lands like a punch.

ELIPHAZ: THE GLOVES COME OFF

Eliphaz leads again. But the gentle counselor of round one is gone. This time he opens with an insult: "Should a wise man answer with empty talk and fill himself with the hot east wind?" He's calling Job a windbag. Then he gets sharper: "Your sin teaches your mouth. You choose the tongue of the crafty. Your own mouth condemns you, not me."

Do you hear what's happened? In round one, Eliphaz said Job should lean on his integrity and trust that things would get better. Now he's saying Job's words prove he's guilty. Job hasn't committed some new sin between rounds. He's simply refused to accept the friends' diagnosis. And in Eliphaz's mind, that refusal *is* the sin. Rejecting their theology is the same as rejecting God.

Eliphaz then asks a series of sarcastic questions: Were you the first human ever born? Were you there before the mountains? Did you sit in on God's secret council? He's mocking Job for daring to think he knows more than they do. And there's a deep irony here that Eliphaz can't see: Job actually *was* discussed in God's council. The reader knows that. Eliphaz doesn't.

The rest of his speech is a long description of the miserable life of the wicked: a man who shakes his fist at God and lives in constant dread, whose prosperity is temporary and whose end is desolation. Eliphaz never names Job directly. He doesn't need to.

JOB RESPONDS: GOD THE ATTACKER

Job has heard enough. He fires back at all three friends at once, calling them "miserable comforters." He's imagining what it would be like if their roles were reversed—if *they* were the ones suffering and *he* was the one offering advice. He could string together the same empty phrases they use. He could shake his head in disapproval just as easily. But he hopes, if it came to that, he would actually try to help.

Then Job turns from his friends to his real opponent: God. And the language is violent.

God has "torn me in his wrath." God has "gnashed his teeth at me." God "seized me by the neck and dashed me to pieces." God "set me up as his target" and "his archers surround me." God "slashes open my body and does not spare." God "runs at me like a warrior."

These aren't theological statements. They're the cries of a man who feels like God has declared war on him. Job isn't debating a doctrine. He's describing what his life feels like from the inside. And what it feels like is an ambush.

But then—right in the middle of this torrent of anguish— something astonishing happens. Job suddenly says, "Even now my witness is in heaven; my advocate is on high. My intercessor is my friend as my eyes pour out tears to God; he pleads with God on behalf of a man as one pleads for a friend."

Where did that come from? In the first cycle, Job wished for an "umpire" who could stand between him and God. Now the wish has grown into something closer to faith. Somewhere—he doesn't know where, he can't explain how—Job senses that there is someone in the heavenly court who is on his side. Not an enemy. A friend. A witness who will speak for him even after he's gone.

The glimpse vanishes almost as quickly as it appears. But it's there. And it will come back.

BILDAD: SHORTER AND SHARPER

Bildad's second speech is almost a copy of Eliphaz's, another extended picture of the doom that awaits the wicked. But his language is more personal. He describes a man whose "light is darkened in his tent" and whose "lamp above him is put out." Disease eats his skin. He is torn from the safety of his home and marched before "the king of terrors." His memory is erased from the earth. He has no children, no survivors, no legacy.

The cruelty isn't just in the imagery. It's in the fact that Bildad is describing, point by point, exactly what has already happened to Job and presenting it as proof that Job deserved it.

JOB'S GREATEST SPEECH: I KNOW MY REDEEMER LIVES

Job's response to Bildad is one of the most emotionally wrenching passages in all of Scripture. It swings from the lowest low to the highest high in the span of a few verses.

He begins in despair. God has wronged me. He has stripped me of my honor. He has uprooted my hope like a tree. My relatives have gone away. My closest friends have forgotten me. My servants treat me like a stranger. My wife finds me repulsive. Even little children mock me. He is utterly, completely alone.

Then comes the plea that would break anyone's heart: "Have pity on me, have pity on me, O you my friends, for the hand of God has touched me! Why do you pursue me as God does?"

He's begging. The man who once was the greatest in all the East is on his knees in the ashes, asking the friends who are supposed to be comforting him to just stop hurting him for one second.

And then it happens. From somewhere deeper than reason, deeper than theology, deeper than anything his circumstances could possibly justify, Job finds words that have echoed across three thousand years: "I know that my Redeemer lives, and that in the end he will stand upon the earth. And after my skin has been destroyed, yet in my flesh I will see God; I myself will see him with my own eyes—I, and not another. How my heart yearns within me!"

This is not a calm, collected doctrinal statement. This is a man drowning who suddenly, impossibly, grabs hold of something solid. Job has gone from wishing for an umpire, to imagining a witness in heaven, to declaring with ferocious certainty: my Redeemer *lives*. The God who seems to be my enemy is actually my closest relative: the one whose duty it is to defend me, to avenge my honor, to set the record straight. And I will see him. Not through someone else's eyes. Mine.

We need to be honest about what Job means here. He isn't predicting Jesus, at least not directly. He isn't talking about resurrection the way Christians understand it. He's reaching for something he can barely see: a future moment when God himself will stand up, speak the truth about Job, and vindicate him before the watching world. But even if Job doesn't fully understand what he's glimpsing, the trajectory of his hope points forward toward a Redeemer who really does live, who really did stand on this earth, and who really will set all things right.

ZOPHAR: DRIPPING WITH VENOM

Zophar's second speech is the most vicious of the cycle. He describes a wicked man who gorges himself on sin the way a glutton gorges on food, and then God makes him vomit it all up. Wealth that was swallowed will be disgorged. The venom of serpents will course through him. He will never enjoy the rivers flowing with honey and cream. Fire will consume his tent. Heaven and earth will testify against him.

Every metaphor is aimed at Job. Every image is designed to make him confess. Zophar is no longer even trying to comfort. He's trying to crush.

JOB TURNS THE TABLES

Job's final speech of the second cycle changes the game. Instead of defending his innocence yet again, he goes on the offensive. He tells the friends to look around—really look—at the world they actually live in.

The wicked prosper. Their homes are safe. Their livestock multiply. Their children dance and sing. They live out their years in comfort and go down to the grave in peace. They spend their whole lives telling God, "Leave us alone. We don't want to know your ways," and nothing bad ever happens to them.

Job is dismantling the retribution principle from the other side. The friends keep saying the wicked are punished.

Job says: show me. Where is the evidence? Go ask anyone on the street. Evil people are spared on the day of disaster. They are buried with honor. Crowds follow their funeral processions.

Then comes the gut punch: "So how can you console me with empty nonsense? Your answers are nothing but lies."

Job isn't just rejecting the friends' arguments. He's rejecting the entire framework they've been working from. And he's doing it with evidence from the real world that anyone with eyes can see.

WHAT THIS MEANS FOR US

First, people who are hurting need compassion, not theology lessons. The friends had real knowledge. They weren't ignorant. But they used their knowledge as a weapon instead of a bandage. When someone you care about is suffering, the question isn't "What true thing can I say?" It's "What does this person actually need from me right now?"

Second, faith sometimes grows in the darkest places. Job's declaration about his Redeemer didn't come during a worship service or a quiet devotional. It came in the middle of the worst season of his life, surrounded by people who had turned against him, after accusing God of being his enemy. Sometimes the most powerful moments of faith are born not from comfort but from desperation.

Third, beware of systems that explain everything. The retribution principle gave the friends an answer for every situation. And that's exactly what made it dangerous. Any system that always has an answer, that never says "I don't know," that never lets reality challenge its assumptions, will eventually do more harm than good. Real wisdom knows its own limits.

Fourth, it is okay to say that life isn't fair. Job looked at the world and saw wicked people thriving and righteous people suffering, and he said so out loud. The Bible doesn't rebuke him for that observation. Sometimes the most faithful thing you can do is tell the truth about what you see, even when it doesn't fit the story everyone else is telling.

TALKING POINTS

1. **The friends shifted from offering advice to painting terrifying pictures of the fate of the wicked.** Why do you think their tone changed so much between rounds? What does it tell us about what happens when people feel their worldview is being threatened?

2. **Job called his friends "miserable comforters."** What's the difference between a comforter and a lecturer? When someone is suffering, how do you know which role to play?

3. **Job's declaration "I know that my Redeemer lives" is one of the most famous lines in the Bible.** What makes it so powerful that it came in the middle of such total despair rather than in a moment of peace?

4. **Job argued that the wicked often prosper while the righteous suffer.** Is that true in your experience? How do you handle it when life seems unfair and the wrong people seem to win?

5. **The friends were absolutely certain they were right.** Job was absolutely certain he was innocent. Is it possible for both sides in an argument to be partly right and partly wrong?

What would it have taken for someone in this story to say, "I don't know"?

Round two is over. The friends have thrown everything they have at Job, and he hasn't budged. The retribution principle is cracking under the weight of reality. And somewhere in the rubble, a small, stubborn flame of hope is still burning. But the debate isn't done. There's one more round—and this time, things are going to fall apart.

Turn the page.

5

WHEN THE OTHER SIDE GOES QUIET

Have you ever been in an argument—a real one, not just a small disagreement—where you knew you were right, and the other person knew it too, but they just couldn't bring themselves to admit it?

Maybe it was with a sibling. They accused you of something. You denied it. They pushed harder. You pushed back. They got louder. You got firmer. And then, gradually, something shifted. Their voice got less confident. Their accusations started to repeat. They ran out of new things to say. Eventually they either changed the subject, muttered something under their breath, or just walked away. Not because the argument was resolved, but because they had nothing left.

There's a strange satisfaction in that moment, but also a strange emptiness. You won, sort of. But nobody actually learned anything. Nobody changed their mind. The argument just… collapsed under its own weight.

That's exactly what happens in the third round of speeches in Job. For two full cycles, Eliphaz, Bildad, and Zophar have hammered Job with the same basic argument: you're suffering because you sinned. Repent and God will restore you. Job has refused, again and again, insisting on his innocence and demanding answers from God. And now, in round three, the cracks in the friends' case become fractures—and then the whole structure caves in.

Eliphaz gives one final speech. Bildad manages only six verses. Zophar doesn't say a word.

The debate is falling apart. And the collapse itself is making a point.

ELIPHAZ: INVENTING SINS

Eliphaz goes first, as always. But this time he's done being subtle. In round one, he hinted that Job might have some hidden failing. In round two, he described the fate of the wicked and let Job draw the connection. Now, in round three, he drops all pretense and directly accuses Job of specific sins. "Is not your wickedness great? There is no end to your iniquities."

And then comes a list: You've demanded collateral from your brothers for debts they don't owe. You've refused water to the thirsty and bread to the hungry. You've sent widows away empty-handed. You've crushed orphans.

Here's the thing: none of this is true. Not a word. The reader knows it. God himself declared Job blameless in the opening chapters. Eliphaz has no evidence for any of these charges. He's not reporting what he's seen. He's manufacturing a case that fits his theory.

This is what happens when a system becomes more important than the truth. The retribution principle says suffering equals sin. Job is suffering. Therefore Job has sinned. If there's no visible sin, then the sin must be invisible. And if the invisible sin can't be found, it must be invented. Eliphaz has reasoned his way from a theology into a lie.

After the accusations, Eliphaz offers one more appeal. Return to God, he says. Agree with him. Be at peace. Let him be your treasure instead of gold. Pray, and he'll hear you. Make promises, and you'll fulfill them. Light will shine on your path again.

It's a beautiful invitation—and it's built on a rotten foundation. Eliphaz is offering Job a deal: confess sins you didn't commit, and God will make your life nice again. It's the retribution principle dressed up as spiritual advice. And it reveals what Eliphaz has believed all along: that the relationship between God and humans is fundamentally transactional. You give God what he wants, and he gives you what you want. Do the right things, get the right results.

Job isn't buying it.

JOB RESPONDS: IF ONLY I COULD FIND HIM

Job's response to Eliphaz is one of the most honest prayers in the Bible, even though it's not exactly a prayer. It's more like thinking out loud, wrestling with the terrifying reality of a God who seems to be everywhere and nowhere at the same time.

"Oh, that I knew where to find him, that I could go to where he lives! I would state my case before him and fill my mouth with arguments."

This is Job's deepest longing. Not for his wealth back. Not for his health back. Not even for his children back. What he wants more than anything is to stand face to face with God and make his case. He's convinced that if he could just get a hearing—a real one, not filtered through the friends' broken theology—God would listen. God wouldn't overpower him. God would actually pay attention.

Then comes one of the most striking lines in the book: "He knows the way that I take; when he has tested me, I will come forth as gold." That's not arrogance. That's the stubborn confidence of a man who knows he's been living with integrity and refuses to pretend otherwise, no matter how much pressure his friends pile on. Job isn't claiming to be perfect. He's claiming to be honest. And he trusts that God—the real God, not the vending machine God of the friends' theology—knows the difference.

But the confidence doesn't last. Job looks around and can't find God anywhere. East, west, north, south. Nothing. And the thought creeps back in: God can do whatever he wants, and no one can stop him. "He carries out his decree against me, and many such plans he still has in store. That is why I am terrified before him."

Job is caught between two realities he can't reconcile. He believes God is just. He believes he himself is innocent. And he can see with his own eyes that the world is full of wicked people getting away with murder—literally. He describes them in vivid detail in chapter 24: people who move boundary stones to steal land, who drive away the orphan's donkey, who force the poor to hide in the wilderness like wild animals, who strip the naked of their clothing, who murder in the darkness.

Where is God in all of this? Why doesn't he hold court? Why aren't there set times when the wicked are brought to account? Job isn't just asking about his own case anymore. He's asking about the world.

BILDAD: RUNNING ON EMPTY

And then it's Bildad's turn. In round one, he spoke for twenty-two verses. In round two, he managed eighteen. Now, in round three, he offers six.

Six verses. That's it. He doesn't accuse Job of anything specific. He doesn't describe the fate of the wicked. He doesn't even address Job's arguments. He just makes one small, tired point: God is powerful. The moon isn't bright enough for him. The stars aren't pure in his eyes. How much less a human being, who is nothing but a maggot? A worm?

It's a pale echo of what Eliphaz said in round one, that no mortal can be pure before God. But where Eliphaz built a whole argument around the idea, Bildad just states it and sits down. He's got nothing left. The tank is empty. The argument that was supposed to crush Job has run out of fuel.

ZOPHAR: SILENCE

Zophar doesn't speak at all. In round one, he was the harshest of the three, telling Job that God was actually going easy on him. In round two, he painted a grotesque picture of the wicked man choking on his own sin. Now? Nothing. Not a word.

The silence is deafening. And it's not a respectful silence, like the seven days at the beginning. It's the silence of a man who has been defeated by reality. Zophar has nothing more to say because his system has nothing more to offer. When your only tool is a hammer, and the nail refuses to go in, eventually you just stop swinging.

The collapse of the third cycle isn't just a literary curiosity. It's making a theological point: human wisdom has hit a wall.

Three of the wisest men in the ancient world have thrown everything they have at Job's situation, and they've failed. Their theology couldn't explain it. Their arguments couldn't sustain it. Their accusations couldn't prove it. The retribution principle, applied rigidly and without mercy, has been weighed and found wanting.

Something else will have to speak.

JOB: I WILL NOT DENY MY INTEGRITY

With the friends sputtering out, Job takes the floor, and he doesn't waste the moment. His response to Bildad is dripping with sarcasm: "How you have helped the powerless! How you have saved the arm that is feeble! What advice you have offered to one without wisdom!"

Then he pivots to something unexpected. Instead of attacking God again, Job describes God's power over creation, and he does it with genuine awe. God stretches out the heavens over empty space. He wraps up water in his clouds. He stirs up the sea and strikes down the ancient chaos monsters. The pillars of heaven tremble at his rebuke.

But here's the kicker. After this breathtaking description of divine power, Job says: "And these are but the outer fringe of his works; how faint the whisper we hear of him! Who then can understand the thunder of his power?"

Everything the friends have said about God, everything Job himself has said—all of it is just the faintest whisper of who God actually is. Nobody in this debate has come close to understanding the full reality. The friends haven't. Job hasn't. No human being can. God is bigger than every box anyone has tried to put him in.

And then, with the friends silent and the debate crumbling, Job delivers the most powerful oath in the entire book. He swears by the living God—the very God he's been arguing with—that he will never, ever concede that the friends are right.

"As long as I have life within me, as long as the breath of God is in my nostrils, my lips will not say anything wicked, and my tongue will not utter lies. I will never admit you are in the right; till I die, I will not deny my integrity. I will maintain my innocence and never let go of it; my conscience will not reproach me as long as I live."

This is Job's line in the sand. He's not budging. Not for the friends, not for the pressure, not for the theology, not even for the pain. His integrity is the one thing he has left, and he will hold onto it with both hands until his last breath.

Notice what's happening here. The friends have spent three rounds trying to get Job to let go of his righteousness. To confess, to repent, to admit the system works. Job has spent three rounds refusing. And by refusing, by maintaining his integrity even when everything in his world screams at him to give it up, Job is actually proving the point of the entire book. The accuser asked, "Does Job fear God for nothing?" Job's answer, forged in three rounds of fire, is yes.

He just doesn't know it yet.

WHAT THIS MEANS FOR US

First, when people invent evidence to support their theory, the theory is the problem. Eliphaz couldn't find real sins in Job's life, so he made some up. Whenever you find yourself or someone else stretching the truth to make a system work, that's a sign the system needs to be questioned, not the person being forced into it.

Second, wanting to meet God face to face is one of the deepest human longings. Job didn't want explanations from friends or comfort from theology. He wanted God himself. That desire—to stand before God and be truly known—is planted in every human heart. And the good news of the Bible is that God eventually answers it, not with a courtroom hearing, but with a person: Jesus, who is called Immanuel, "God with us."

Third, there is a kind of silence that means something has broken. Zophar's silence isn't peace. It's defeat. When a worldview can't hold the weight of someone's real suffering, it will eventually go quiet. Pay attention to what stops being said. It often tells you more than what's still being argued.

Fourth, integrity is not the same as perfection. Job never claimed to be sinless. What he claimed was that he hadn't done anything to deserve what happened to him, and that he refused to lie about it. Integrity isn't about being flawless. It's about being honest—with yourself, with others, and with God—even when honesty costs you everything.

TALKING POINTS

1. **Eliphaz invented specific sins to accuse Job of, things like refusing water to the thirsty and crushing orphans.** Why do you think he did that? What does it reveal about what happens when a person's theology matters more to them than the truth?

2. **Job said, "When he has tested me, I will come forth as gold."** What does that metaphor mean? How does fire re-

fine gold, and what does that tell us about how suffering might work in a person's life?

3. **Bildad's speech shrank from twenty-two verses in round one to six verses in round three. Zophar said nothing at all.** What do you think their silence means? Have you ever been in a situation where you realized you had nothing left to say?

4. **Job swore he would never deny his integrity, even if it meant dying.** Is there anything in your life that you would hold onto no matter what, even if everyone around you told you to let it go? What gives a person that kind of determination?

5. **Job described God's power in creation and then said, "These are but the outer fringe of his works."** What does it mean that everything we know about God is just a "faint whisper"? How should that change the way we talk about God and about other people's suffering?

The human voices are nearly spent. The friends have exhausted their arguments. Job has defended his innocence to the breaking point. But before anyone else speaks, the book pauses, and a poem about wisdom drops into the silence like a stone into still water.

Turn the page.

6

THE ONE THING YOU CAN'T GOOGLE

Have you ever tried to search for the answer to a question that really mattered—not a homework question or a trivia fact, but something deep—and realized there was no website, no video, no book that could give you what you were looking for?

Maybe someone you loved got sick, and you wanted to know *why*. Not what the diagnosis was; you could look that up. But *why them*? Why now? You typed your question into a search bar and got medical articles, statistics, survivor stories. All useful, but none of them the answer you actually needed.

Or maybe your parents split up, and you wanted to understand how two people who once loved each other could stop. You could read a hundred articles about divorce and still not have the answer, because the answer you wanted wasn't information. It was understanding. And understanding isn't something you can dig up like a buried treasure, no matter how hard you look.

That's the experience Job 28 is about. It's a poem, one of the most beautiful in the entire Bible. And it asks a single, haunting question: *Where can wisdom be found?*

Not knowledge. Not facts. Not data. *Wisdom.* The deep understanding of how the world actually works and why things happen the way they do. The kind of understanding that could make sense of everything Job has been through.

And the poem's answer will change the direction of the entire book.

A PAUSE IN THE STORM

Before we look at the poem itself, notice where it falls. The three rounds of debate are over. The friends have exhausted their arguments. Bildad barely spoke in round three, and Zophar didn't speak at all. Job has defended his innocence to the breaking point. The air is still thick with accusations and counterarguments and pain.

And then, like a clearing in the middle of a forest, this poem appears.

Many scholars believe Job 28 isn't spoken by Job or the friends or even Elihu. It may be the voice of the narrator, the author of the book stepping forward for a moment to offer a comment before the story moves on. Think of it as the camera pulling back from the argument to show you the bigger picture. The characters are too close to the problem to see it clearly. The narrator can see what they can't.

And what the narrator wants you to understand is this: everything you've just heard—three rounds of the best human thinking the ancient world could produce—hasn't come close to real wisdom. Not one word of it.

DIGGING FOR TREASURE

The poem begins with an image that would have fascinated ancient readers: mining.

Human beings are astonishingly resourceful. They dig shafts into the earth, far from civilization, descending into total darkness. They blast through rock with fire. They dam up rivers and reroute streams. They hang from ropes in pitch-black tunnels, swinging over nothing, searching for veins of silver and gold and sapphire hidden deep underground. No bird of prey can spot these places from above. No lion has ever set foot on these paths. Only humans go there, driven by determination and hunger for what's hidden.

And they find it. That's the point. Humans can penetrate the deepest, darkest, most inaccessible places on earth and bring hidden treasures into the light. When it comes to the physical world, there is almost nothing we can't figure out if we try hard enough.

But then the poem pivots with a question that stops everything cold: "But where can wisdom be found? Where does understanding dwell?"

WHAT MONEY CAN'T BUY

The answer, at first, is entirely negative. Wisdom is not in the land of the living. The Deep says, "It's not in me." The Sea says, "It's not with me." You can search every corner of the earth—the highest mountains, the deepest oceans, the farthest reaches of exploration—and you will not find it.

And you can't buy it, either. The poem rolls out a dazzling list of the most precious materials the ancient world knew:

gold, silver, the gold of Ophir, onyx, sapphire, crystal, coral, pearls, topaz. All of them rare. All of them stunningly beautiful. All of them the product of the kind of human ingenuity the first section just celebrated.

None of them is worth enough.

Wisdom cannot be purchased at any price. You can't trade for it. You can't earn it. You can't dig it out of the ground, no matter how deep you go. Every treasure humanity has ever unearthed, stacked together, would not be enough to buy a single glimpse of the wisdom that explains how the world really works.

The question repeats: "Where then does wisdom come from? Where does understanding dwell?"

Even the realm of the dead can't help. Destruction and Death themselves—personified here as if they're ancient beings who have existed since the beginning—say, "We've heard a rumor of it, but that's all." Even the underworld, the place humans fear most, catches only the faintest echo of wisdom. It doesn't live there either.

So where is it?

GOD ALONE

The answer arrives in verse 23, and it's simple and enormous: "God understands the way to it, and he alone knows where it dwells."

God sees to the ends of the earth. He looks under the whole heaven. He established the weight of the wind and measured out the waters. He set the rules for the rain and charted the path of the thunderstorm. When he created the world, he didn't work blindly. He used wisdom. He saw it, examined it, established it, tested it. Wisdom was the blueprint. The cosmos was the building.

This means something profound for the debate we've been reading. Job's friends tried to explain the world using a formula: righteousness equals blessing, wickedness equals suffering. Job tried to explain the world by accusing God of injustice. Both approaches assumed that human beings could figure out the operating system of the universe if they just thought hard enough.

The poem says: no, you can't. The wisdom behind how the world works belongs to God alone. Humans can mine silver. They can split rock. They can explore the ocean floor. But the wisdom that governs why things happen the way they do—why the righteous sometimes suffer, why the wicked sometimes prosper, why the rain falls where no one lives, why a good man loses everything for no apparent reason—that wisdom is not available for human discovery. It's God's. It always has been.

SO WHAT DO WE GET?

If the poem ended at verse 27, it would be beautiful but devastating. We would be left with nothing: a universe governed by a wisdom we can never access, run by a God whose reasons we can never know.

But the poem doesn't end there. Verse 28 gives us something: "And he said to all humanity: 'The fear of the Lord—that is wisdom, and to turn away from evil is understanding.'"

This is not the cosmic, blueprint-of-the-universe wisdom that governs creation. That kind of wisdom remains God's alone. But there is a wisdom available to human beings, and it's defined in the simplest possible terms: take God seriously, and live accordingly.

The fear of the Lord isn't terror. It's not running from God or cringing before him. It's the posture of a creature who recognizes that the Creator is infinitely greater, infinitely wiser, and infinitely more capable of running the world than they are. It's humility. Not the fake kind that puts itself down, but the real kind that knows its place. It's the decision to trust that God is wise even when his wisdom makes no sense to you.

And notice what this verse echoes. All the way back in chapter 1, the narrator described Job as a man who "feared God and turned away from evil." The poem is gently pointing back to who Job was before the catastrophe. That's who he needs to become again, not by pretending the suffering didn't happen, but by letting go of his demand to understand *why* it happened and choosing instead to trust the God whose wisdom is beyond his reach.

Job isn't there yet. He'll need a few more chapters, and a voice from a whirlwind, before he gets there. But the poem has planted the seed.

WHAT THIS MEANS FOR US

First, there are questions that human beings simply cannot answer. Not because we're not smart enough, and not because we haven't tried hard enough, but because the answers belong to a level of wisdom that is God's alone. "Why did this happen to me?" may be a question without a human answer, and that's not a failure of faith. It's a recognition of reality.

Second, wisdom is not the same as information. We live in a world that can answer almost any factual question in seconds. But the deepest questions—Why is life unfair? Why do good people suffer? What is the point of all this?—aren't factual questions. They're wisdom questions. And wisdom doesn't come from a search engine. It comes from a relationship with the God who built the world.

Third, the fear of the Lord is the starting point, not the finish line. Fearing God doesn't mean you instantly understand everything. It means you've chosen the right posture—humble, trusting, open—from which real understanding can eventually grow. It's the foundation, not the roof.

Fourth, sometimes the bravest thing a book can say is "we don't know yet." The poem doesn't answer the question of why Job is suffering. It doesn't vindicate Job or condemn the friends. It simply says: the wisdom you're all looking for is beyond human reach. Stop trying to master it and start trusting the One who holds it. That's not a cop-out. That's the deepest thing any of the speakers in this book has said so far.

TALKING POINTS

1. **The poem celebrates human ability (mining, exploring, discovering) and then says wisdom is the one thing we can't dig up.** Why do you think the author chose mining as the comparison? What does it tell us about the difference between knowledge and wisdom?

2. **Wisdom can't be purchased with gold, silver, or gems.** Can you think of other things in life that money can't buy?

Why is it so hard for people to accept that some things are simply beyond their reach?

3. **The poem says that even Destruction and Death have only "heard a rumor" of wisdom.** What does that image suggest about how far removed true wisdom is from anything in the created world?

4. **"The fear of the Lord—that is wisdom."** What does it mean to "fear" God in a way that isn't about being scared? How is that kind of fear different from what Job's friends were telling him to do?

5. **This poem comes right after the debate collapsed.** Why do you think the author placed it here? What effect does it have on how you read everything that came before and everything that's about to come?

The poem has spoken. The debate is over. But Job isn't finished. He has one more speech to make, and it's not a debate anymore. It's a final, defiant statement of everything he's lost, everything he's suffered, and everything he still believes about himself. Job is about to rest his case.

Turn the page.

7

THE CLOSING ARGUMENT

Have you ever scrolled through old photos on your phone—pictures from a birthday party, a family vacation, a random Tuesday when everyone you loved was in the same room laughing—and felt something twist in your chest?

Not just nostalgia. Something sharper. Because the people in those pictures aren't all in your life the same way anymore. Maybe your parents split up. Maybe your best friend moved away. Maybe someone got sick. Maybe *you* changed, and the kid in those photos feels like a stranger. The pictures haven't changed, but your life has, and the distance between then and now hits you like a wave you didn't see coming.

Everyone has a "before." A time when things felt right, or at least felt normal. And when that time ends, whether it ends slowly or all at once, you carry the memory of it like a bruise that won't stop being tender.

That's where Job is in chapters 29–31. The debate is over. The friends have gone quiet. The wisdom poem has spoken its piece. And now, alone in the silence, Job does something he hasn't done in the entire book: he looks backward, he looks at the present, and then he looks God in the eye and says, "Your move."

This is Job's closing argument. And it's devastating.

CHAPTER 29: THE WAY THINGS WERE

Job begins by remembering. "Oh, that I were as in the months of old, as in the days when God watched over me, when his lamp shone upon my head, and by his light I walked through darkness."

What follows is the most detailed portrait of Job's former life anywhere in the book. We knew from chapter 1 that he was wealthy and righteous. But chapter 29 fills in the picture with color and warmth and human detail.

Job remembers the friendship of God over his tent. Not just God's blessing, but his *presence*, his closeness, the sense that the Creator of the universe was personally invested in Job's daily life. He remembers his children around him. He remembers abundance so rich that it felt like his feet were washed in cream and the rocks poured out streams of olive oil.

But what Job remembers most vividly isn't his wealth. It's his honor.

When he walked to the city gate—the place where leaders gathered to settle disputes and make decisions—young men stepped aside out of respect. Old men stood up when he entered. Princes stopped talking and put their hands over their mouths. Nobles went silent. Not because they were afraid of him, but because they respected him so deeply that they wanted-ed to hear what he would say.

And why did they respect him? Because of how he treated people. He rescued the poor who cried for help. He defended the orphan who had no one. He made widows' hearts sing for joy. He was "eyes to the blind and feet to the lame." He investigated the cases of strangers he'd never met and broke the power of those who exploited the weak.

Job clothed himself in righteousness, he says, "and it clothed me. My justice was like a robe and a turban." He wore his integrity the way a king wears a crown: not as a performance, but as an identity. It was who he was.

And he expected to die that way. "I thought, 'I will die in my nest, and I will multiply my days like sand.'" He pictured himself growing old in comfort, surrounded by family, his roots spread toward the water, his glory fresh, his strength unbroken. He would die honored. He would die whole.

That was the before.

CHAPTER 30: THE WAY THINGS ARE

The word "but" at the beginning of chapter 30 hits like a door slamming. "But now they laugh at me—men younger than I, whose fathers I would have disdained to put with the dogs that guarded my flock."

The reversal is total. The man once honored by princes is now mocked by society's outcasts, homeless scavengers who live in caves and eat roots, who have been driven out of civilization and branded as criminals. These are people so low on the social ladder that Job wouldn't have let their fathers near his livestock. And now *they* look down on *him*. They sing cruel songs about him. They spit in his face.

Then Job turns from the human tormentors to the divine one. "God has thrown me into the mud. I have become like dust and ashes."

The imagery gets violent. God has seized him by his clothing, grabbed him by the collar, and hurled him into the filth. God has turned cruel. God hates him. God lifts him up only to throw him into the storm. And worst of all, when Job cries out for help, God doesn't answer. He just stares. "I cry out to you, but you do not answer me. I stand, and you barely look at me."

Then comes the most heartbreaking contrast in the entire speech. Job reminds God—and anyone listening—that when *other* people were suffering, *he* helped them. "Did I not weep for those whose days were hard? Did I not grieve for the poor?" He did. He was the man who never looked away from someone else's pain. And now that he's the one suffering, nobody—not God, not his friends, not his community—will do for him what he did for everyone else.

His music has turned to mourning. His instrument plays only the sound of weeping.

CHAPTER 31: THE OATH

And then Job does something extraordinary. He stops grieving and starts swearing.

Chapter 31 is a formal oath of innocence, the ancient equivalent of taking the witness stand, putting your hand on a Bible, and swearing to tell the truth. But Job goes further than that. He doesn't just say "I'm innocent." He walks through a comprehensive list of sins and, for each one, calls down a specific curse on himself if he's guilty.

The structure follows a pattern: *If I have done this, then let this terrible thing happen to me.*

If I have lusted after a woman, let God see my steps and judge me.

If I have been dishonest in business, let me be weighed on honest scales and found blameless.

If I have committed adultery, let my own wife be taken from me.

If I have been unjust to my servants, what would I do when God rises up against me? Didn't the same God who made me in the womb make them?

If I have ignored the poor, refused food to the hungry, neglected the orphan, or failed to clothe the naked, let my arm be torn from its socket.

If I have put my trust in gold or worshiped the sun and moon, that would be a crime against the God above.

If I have celebrated when my enemies suffered, or turned a stranger away from my door, or hidden my sins like a coward afraid of what people would think, then let the worst come.

The list is breathtaking. It covers the full range of moral life: sexual ethics, business integrity, treatment of employees, care for the vulnerable, honesty about wealth, faithfulness to God alone, mercy toward enemies, hospitality to strangers, and transparency about failure. Job isn't just claiming to be "pretty good." He's submitting his entire life, every corner of it, to examination and daring God to find a flaw.

What makes this passage remarkable isn't just the breadth of the list. It's the *values* behind it. Job treats his servants as equals before God: "Did not he who made me in the womb make them?" That's a statement about human dignity that was centuries ahead of its time. He refuses to celebrate the downfall of his enemies, a level of moral maturity that most people (ancient or modern) never reach. He rejects the worship of wealth, even though he was once the richest man in the East.

These aren't the values of a man trying to earn God's favor. These are the values of a man who has genuinely internalized what it means to live with integrity, regardless of what he gets in return.

THE SIGNATURE

Then comes the climax. Job breaks off the list of oaths and cries out: "Oh, that I had someone to hear me! Here is my signature—let the Almighty answer me! Let my accuser write out an indictment!"

Job has signed his name. He's put everything on the line. He's not just saying "I'm innocent" in a general way. He's filed a formal legal document and dared God to respond with the charges against him. And if God does produce a document listing Job's sins? Job says he would carry it on his shoulder like a medal and wear it on his head like a crown because he's *that* confident it would vindicate rather than condemn him. He would approach God "like a prince."

Then he falls silent. "The words of Job are ended." The courtroom is quiet. The defense has rested. The defendant has sworn his oath, signed his name, and taken his seat.

Now it's up to the judge to speak.

But there's something the reader should notice before we move on. For all its power and nobility, Job's closing argument has a blind spot. He has described, in magnificent detail, what he did for other people. He has catalogued his moral achievements. He has declared that he lived a life worthy of honor. But in three full chapters, he has not once said, "I need God." He has said he misses God's blessing. He has said he wants God to answer him. He has said God has treated him unfairly. But he has not said, "Even if I never get an answer, even if things never go back to the way they were, God is still worthy of my trust."

Job's integrity is real. His innocence is genuine. But his closing argument reveals something: even a righteous man can stand so tall in his own goodness that he forgets how small he is before God. Job is about to find that out.

WHAT THIS MEANS FOR US

First, it is not wrong to grieve what you've lost. Job's longing for the way things used to be isn't weakness. It's honesty. When life changes for the worse, it's natural and healthy to name what's been taken from you. Grief doesn't mean you've given up. It means the thing you lost was real and good, and you're not pretending otherwise.

Second, true integrity shows up in how you treat people who can't do anything for you. Job's list of moral commitments isn't about rule-following. It's about seeing other people—servants, orphans, widows, strangers, enemies—as fully human and fully worthy of dignity. That's not just ancient wisdom. That's the heart of what Jesus later called the second greatest commandment: love your neighbor as yourself.

Third, there is a difference between defending your innocence and demanding your rights. Job's oath is noble, and the text never says he's wrong about his innocence; he isn't. But there's a subtle shift between "I haven't done anything to deserve this" and "God owes me an explanation." The first is a true statement. The second is a posture that puts Job on the throne and God in the witness box. Sometimes the truest thing about us is also the thing that most needs to be surrendered.

Fourth, signing your name to your life takes courage. Job was willing to have every part of his existence examined: his eyes, his hands, his heart, his wallet, his relationships. Most of us would rather keep a few rooms in the house locked. Job threw open every door. That's the kind of honesty God is looking for, even when it comes with rough edges.

TALKING POINTS

1. **Job described his former life as a time when "the friendship of God was upon my tent."** What do you think it feels like to have that kind of closeness with God? Have you ever experienced something like it and then felt it slip away?

2. **In chapter 30, Job says he wept for those in trouble and grieved for the poor, but now no one does the same for him.** Why is it so painful when the help you gave to others isn't returned? How should we respond when our kindness isn't reciprocated?

3. **Job declared that his servants were made by the same God who made him.** Why was that such a radical statement for his time? What does it mean for how we should treat people today, especially people with less power or status than us?

4. **Job signed his name and challenged God to produce an indictment.** Would you be willing to have your entire life

examined the way Job offered his? What would be the hardest part of that kind of transparency?

5. Job's closing speech is noble and genuine, but it focuses heavily on what Job has done. Is there a danger in being so focused on your own goodness that you forget how much you need God? How do you hold together confidence in your integrity and humility before God?

Job has spoken his last word. His signature is on the table. The courtroom is silent. But someone unexpected is about to break that silence, and it isn't God. Not yet. A young man who's been listening the entire time is about to stand up, furious, and deliver a speech nobody asked for.

Turn the page.

8

THE UNINVITED SPEAKER

Every Sherlock Holmes story follows the same basic pattern. A mystery has stumped everyone. Scotland Yard is baffled, the witnesses are confused, the clues seem to contradict each other. Nobody can figure it out. And then Holmes arrives, surveys the scene, and announces that the answer is obvious. He's usually condescending about it. He explains, in elaborate detail, exactly what everyone else missed and exactly how *he* figured it out. And the maddening thing is, he's usually right. Or at least right enough that everyone has to shut up and listen.

But imagine a Sherlock Holmes who only *thinks* he's cracked the case. Imagine someone who walks into the middle of a mystery that has stumped three experienced investigators and one desperate victim, announces with supreme confidence that he alone has the answer, talks for six chapters straight, gets some things brilliantly right and other things completely wrong, and then sits down to total silence. Nobody responds. Nobody argues. Nobody even acknowledges that he spoke.

That's Elihu.

He appears out of nowhere in chapter 32, a young man who has been sitting on the sidelines for the entire debate, listening to every word the friends and Job have said. He hasn't been introduced. He wasn't mentioned when the friends arrived. He has no backstory, no credentials, and no invitation. But he's been getting angrier and angrier, and now, with Job's oath of innocence ringing in the air and the courtroom waiting for God to respond, Elihu can't hold it in any longer.

He stands up and starts talking. And he doesn't stop for six chapters.

WHY IS HE SO ANGRY?

The narrator tells us Elihu is angry and tells us four times in five verses, just to make sure we don't miss it. He's angry at Job, and he's angry at the three friends, though for very different reasons.

He's angry at Job because, in Elihu's view, Job has been so focused on defending his own righteousness that he's effectively put himself above God. Job has spent the entire debate saying, "I'm right and God is wrong." Elihu finds this insufferable. And on this specific point—that Job has made his own innocence more important than God's character—Elihu actually has a point. God himself will say something very similar in chapter 40.

He's angry at the friends because they failed. They had three rounds of debate to convince Job, and they couldn't do it. Worse, they condemned Job without actually finding any real fault in him. They made accusations based on a theology rather than on evidence, and then they ran out of arguments and went silent. Elihu is frustrated that these supposedly wise men couldn't do better.

So Elihu has positioned himself against everyone. He thinks the friends were incompetent, and he thinks Job is self-righteous. He's the man in the middle, convinced that he's the only one in the room who can see clearly.

"I AM FULL OF WORDS"

Elihu begins with an apology—of sorts. He explains that he's young, and that he held back out of respect for his elders. In ancient culture, that was the expected behavior. Young people listened. Old people spoke. Wisdom came with age.

But Elihu has reached his limit. He's listened to the wisest men available, and none of them could answer Job. So he offers a different basis for his authority: not age or experience, but the spirit within him. It is the breath of God, he says, that gives understanding, not gray hair. Wisdom doesn't automatically come with a long life. It comes from God, and God can give it to the young as easily as to the old.

This is genuinely insightful. It's also breathtakingly arrogant. Elihu is essentially saying, "God has given *me* what he didn't give *you*." Whether that's courage or overconfidence depends entirely on whether he's right.

And then he delivers what might be the most unintentionally funny line in the entire Bible: "I am full of words; the spirit within me compels me. My belly is like wine with no vent, like new wineskins ready to burst. I must speak, that I may find relief."

He's comparing himself to a bottle of wine about to explode.

He physically *cannot* stop himself from talking. The speech has to come out or he'll pop.

It's hard not to smile. But it's also hard not to recognize the type. You've met this person. Maybe you've *been* this person: so full of something you need to say that you can barely wait for the other person to finish before you jump in.

WHAT ELIHU GETS RIGHT

To his credit, Elihu does offer some ideas that none of the other friends raised.

First, he proposes that suffering can be educational. God speaks to people in more ways than one, Elihu says. Sometimes through dreams and visions. Sometimes through pain. Suffering might not be *punishment* for something you did wrong. It might be God's way of *preventing* you from going wrong, or teaching you something you couldn't learn any other way. God "opens people's ears through adversity" and uses affliction to "deliver the afflicted."

This is more sophisticated than anything the three friends said. They had a simple formula: sin leads to suffering. Elihu modifies it: suffering might not be about past sin at all. It might be about future growth. It might be God's classroom, not God's courtroom.

There's something to this. The New Testament will later say that God disciplines those he loves, and that suffering produces perseverance, character, and hope. Elihu isn't completely wrong.

Second, Elihu mentions the possibility of a mediating angel, someone in heaven who can intercede for a suffering person, declare what is right for them, and secure their rescue. This echoes Job's earlier longing for an umpire, a witness, a redeemer—someone to stand between him and God. Elihu's version is different (he imagines an angel rather than God himself), but he's touching the same nerve.

Third, and most importantly, Elihu's accusation that Job has become self-righteous is confirmed by the story itself. Job has been so consumed with proving his own innocence that he's been willing to put God in the wrong to make himself look right. Elihu sees this clearly: "Job has said, 'I am righteous, and God has denied me justice.'" The problem isn't that Job is wrong about his innocence. The problem is that he's made his innocence the most important thing in the universe. More important even than God's wisdom.

WHAT ELIHU GETS WRONG

But for everything Elihu gets right, there's something he gets wrong, or at least something he handles badly.

He still operates within the retribution framework. He's modified it—suffering is discipline rather than punishment—but he still believes that the world runs on a system of divine cause and effect that human beings can understand. This is exactly the assumption that the wisdom poem in chapter 28 challenged: the wisdom behind how God runs the world is not accessible to humans. Elihu thinks he can explain God's system. He can't.

He's also staggeringly self-important. He talks about himself constantly. He demands that people listen to him. He claims to speak "on God's behalf" and to possess "perfect knowledge." He compares himself to a prophet and insists that his words come directly from the Spirit of God. For a young man who just scolded his elders for being arrogant, that's a remarkable lack of self-awareness.

And perhaps most tellingly, he claims to know what Job's problem is, but he gets the diagnosis wrong. He says Job is suffering because God is trying to teach him something, to correct some flaw, to refine his character through the fire. But the reader knows from chapters 1–2 that Job's suffering isn't educational at all. It's a test of whether anyone serves God for nothing. Elihu's answer is more clever than the friends' answer, but it's still the wrong answer, because he's still trying to explain something that doesn't have a human explanation.

THE STORM BUILDS

The most interesting part of Elihu's speech comes at the end, in chapters 36–37, when he stops arguing and starts describing God's power in creation.

He points to the rain, the thunder, the lightning, the snow, the ice, the wind. He describes how God "loads the thick cloud with moisture" and "scatters his lightning." The beasts retreat to their dens. The whirlwind comes from its chamber. The waters freeze. The clouds roll and turn under God's guidance, accomplishing whatever he commands.

Then Elihu turns to Job with a series of questions: "Do you know how God controls the clouds? Can you spread out the skies like he does? Do you know the balancing of the clouds, the wonders of him who is perfect in knowledge?"

These questions sound familiar. They should. They're a preview (a rough draft, almost) of what God himself is about to say from the whirlwind. Elihu is reaching toward the right idea: God is so much greater than anything we can comprehend that demanding an explanation from him is absurd. But Elihu reaches this idea through his own self-importance rather than through genuine humility. He points to the storm and says, "See how much bigger God is than you." God will soon point to the storm and say the same thing, but with a voice that makes Elihu's words sound like a whisper next to a thunderclap.

Some scholars think this final section was meant to be a bridge, that as Elihu describes the gathering storm, the actual storm is rolling in, and by the time Elihu finishes pointing at the clouds, God's voice is already in the thunder.

Whether or not that's exactly how it works, the effect is powerful. Elihu's speech fades into the sound of an approaching tempest. He's been talking about God's power in nature.

He's about to see it firsthand.

THE SILENCE AFTER

And then? Nothing. Nobody responds to Elihu. Job doesn't answer him. The friends don't comment. God doesn't address him when he finally speaks.

What are we supposed to make of that silence?

Some people read it as confirmation. Elihu was right, and there was nothing to argue with. Others read it as dismissal: Elihu was so off-base that nobody bothered engaging. The truth is probably somewhere in between. Elihu was closer to the truth than the three friends in some ways, but he was still trying to do the one thing the entire book has been warning against: explain God's ways with human wisdom.

The wisdom poem in chapter 28 said it clearly: the deep wisdom that governs how God runs the world belongs to God alone. Elihu, for all his spiritual energy and genuine insights, is still a human being trying to crack a code that wasn't designed to be cracked.

He's the last human voice before God speaks. And after God speaks, nothing any human said will sound quite the same.

WHAT THIS MEANS FOR US

First, being partly right is not the same as being right. Elihu nails some things: Job's self-righteousness, the educational potential of suffering, the greatness of God. But he wraps these insights in so much self-importance and misapplied theology that the good parts get buried. Having a true insight doesn't automatically mean your whole framework is correct.

Second, young people can see things that older people miss, but youth is not a credential. Elihu was right that wisdom doesn't belong exclusively to the elderly. God can speak through anyone. But "the spirit compels me" is not a substitute for humility. Feeling strongly that you're right isn't the same as being right. Confidence is not the same as wisdom.

Third, the idea that all suffering is a lesson can be just as harmful as the idea that all suffering is punishment. If you tell someone who is suffering that God is "teaching them something," you're still trying to explain their pain with a formula. Sometimes the most honest response is to sit with the mystery rather than assign it a purpose.

Fourth, sometimes the best thing about a speech is what comes after it. Elihu's greatest contribution to the book of Job might not be anything he said. It might be the fact that his words trail off just as the real storm arrives. He pointed at the sky and said, "God is in there." He was right. And the voice from the whirlwind is about to prove it.

TALKING POINTS

1. **Elihu was angry at both Job and the friends.** Do you think his anger was justified? Is there ever a right time to be angry at people who are arguing, even if both sides have some truth?

2. **Elihu claimed that God gave him special understanding even though he was young.** Do you think young people can sometimes see spiritual truths that older people miss? What are the dangers of claiming that God has given you a special message?

3. **Elihu suggested that suffering might be God's way of teaching us something.** Do you think that's true sometimes? Is it always true? How can you tell the difference between suffering that shapes you and suffering that simply hurts?

4. **Nobody responded to Elihu's speech.** If you were Job, sitting in the ashes after six chapters of a young man telling you what's wrong with you, how would you have reacted?

5. **Elihu's description of the storm in chapters 36–37 sounds a lot like what God will say in chapters 38–41.** What's the difference between a human being pointing at God's power and God himself showing up in that power?

The last human voice has spoken. Every argument has been made. Every angle has been tried. Three friends, one young man, and Job himself have all spent their words, and none of them found the answer. Now the storm is here. And this time, it isn't Elihu talking about thunder. It *is* the thunder.

Turn the page.

9

THE VOICE IN THE STORM

There's a moment in *Bambi* that changes the entire feel of the film. Bambi is young, still learning to walk, still hiding behind his mother. The meadow is beautiful. The forest is safe. Everything is small and manageable and warm.

And then, without warning, his father appears.

The Great Prince of the Forest doesn't announce himself. He doesn't explain who he is or why he's come. He simply steps out of the mist—enormous, silent, his antlers reaching toward the sky like the branches of a tree. Every animal in the meadow goes still. Bambi stares, wide-eyed, unable to speak. His mother whispers, "He is very brave and very wise. That is why he is known as the Great Prince of the Forest."

The Great Prince doesn't speak to Bambi in that scene. He doesn't bend down to the fawn's level or offer comfort or explanation. He is simply *there*—vast, majestic, beyond anything Bambi has encountered. And in that moment, Bambi's world gets bigger. Everything he thought he understood about the forest—the flowers, the butterflies, the playful rabbits—is suddenly set against a backdrop of something immeasurably greater than himself.

That's what happens in Job 38. After thirty-seven chapters of human voices arguing, accusing, defending, and demanding—after friends who talked too much and a young man who talked even more—the voice that everyone has been waiting for finally speaks.

God answers Job out of the whirlwind.

And nothing will ever be the same.

"WHO IS THIS?"

God's opening words are not gentle. They are not comforting. They are not an apology or an explanation. They are a challenge.

"Who is this that darkens my counsel with words without knowledge? Brace yourself like a man; I will question you, and you shall answer me."

After thirty-five chapters of Job demanding answers from God, God flips the script entirely. *He* will ask the questions. *Job* will answer.

And the first question lands like a thunderclap: "Where were you when I laid the foundation of the earth? Tell me, if you understand."

THE FIRST SPEECH: A TOUR OF THE COSMOS

What follows is one of the most breathtaking passages in all of literature. God takes Job on a tour of creation, not to show off, but to show Job how much he doesn't know.

Did you set the dimensions of the earth? Were you there when the morning stars sang together and the angels shouted for joy?

Have you ever commanded the morning? Have you told the dawn where to stand?

Have you walked on the floor of the ocean? Have you seen the gates of death?

Do you know where light comes from? Can you trace the path of darkness back to its home?

Have you entered the storehouses of snow? Have you seen where the hail is kept?

Can you guide the constellations through the sky? Do you know the laws that govern the heavens?

The questions come in wave after wave, and every single one has the same answer: no. No, Job hasn't done any of these things. No, Job doesn't understand how any of this works. No, Job was not there.

But notice something crucial. God isn't just saying "I'm bigger than you." He's showing Job that the cosmos is incomprehensibly complex. Far more complex than any formula can contain. The rain doesn't fall only on the righteous. It falls on deserts where no one lives, watering land that benefits no human being at all. God sends rain where it serves no human purpose, simply because the world is bigger than human purposes.

That detail matters. The friends built their entire theology on the assumption that the world runs on a system of reward and punishment, that everything God does is aimed at humans and can be decoded by humans. God is quietly dismantling that assumption. The universe is not a vending machine that dispenses justice. It's a living, breathing, wildly complex creation governed by a wisdom so far beyond human comprehension that even the edges of it are staggering.

THE ANIMALS

Then God turns from the cosmos to the animal kingdom, and the tour gets personal.

Do you hunt prey for the lioness? Do you feed the ravens when their young cry out in hunger?

Do you know when mountain goats give birth? Do you watch over the deer in labor?

Who let the wild donkey go free? Who gave the ostrich her wings, and then let her be foolish enough to leave her eggs in the sand?

Did you give the horse his strength? Does the hawk soar by your wisdom? Does the eagle build its nest on the heights because you told it to?

What's striking about this parade of creatures is how many of them are useless to humans. The wild donkey won't carry your bags. The ostrich can't think straight. The mountain goat gives birth on a cliff where nobody can watch. These animals don't serve human purposes. They exist because God delights in them, because his creation is not a machine designed for human benefit, but a wild, teeming, extravagant world that runs on his wisdom and reflects his character.

And if God manages all of *this*—every raindrop, every constellation, every lioness with cubs—then maybe, just maybe, he's managing Job's situation too, even when Job can't see it.

JOB'S FIRST RESPONSE: SILENCE

God pauses. And Job—the man who has talked for thirty-five chapters, who has demanded a hearing, who signed his name and dared God to respond—says this: "I am unworthy. How can I reply to you? I put my hand over my mouth. I spoke once, but I have no answer—twice, but I will say no more."

It's not much. It's not repentance. It's not understanding. It's simply a man who has run out of words. The sheer scale of what God has just described has overwhelmed him. Job is like Bambi staring at the Great Prince, suddenly aware that the world is far bigger, and he is far smaller, than he ever imagined.

But God isn't finished.

THE SECOND SPEECH: THE HEART OF THE MATTER

God speaks again from the whirlwind, and this time he goes straight to the center of the problem. "Would you discredit my justice? Would you condemn me to justify yourself?"

There it is. The question that cuts through everything. Job has spent the entire book insisting that *he* is right, which means *God* must be wrong. He has built his case on his own innocence—and his innocence is real. But in defending it, he crossed a line. He didn't just say, "I don't deserve this." He said, "God is unjust." He put himself on the throne and God in the dock.

God challenges him directly: if you think you can do a better job running the world, go ahead. Put on the robes of majesty. Clothe yourself with glory. Pour out your anger on every proud and wicked person. Crush evil wherever you find it. Bury the wicked in the dust. If you can do all that, then I'll admit that your own right hand can save you.

The point isn't that God is bullying Job. The point is that *dealing with evil is harder than Job thinks*. Job has been treating the problem of evil as though it has a simple solution: if God were paying attention, he'd reward the righteous and punish the wicked, and everything would be neat and tidy. God is saying: it's not that simple. The forces of disorder and chaos in this world are real and powerful, and managing them requires a wisdom that no human being possesses.

BEHEMOTH AND LEVIATHAN

And then, to drive the point home, God describes two creatures that have puzzled readers for centuries: Behemoth and Leviathan.

Behemoth is a massive land creature. It eats grass like an ox, but its strength is in its loins and the muscles of its belly. Its tail is like a cedar tree. Its bones are like tubes of bronze and bars of iron. It is the first of God's great works, and only its Maker can approach it with a sword.

Leviathan is even more terrifying. It is a sea creature of almost unimaginable power. Its back is covered with rows of shields sealed tight together. Fire and smoke pour from its mouth and nostrils. No sword, spear, dart, or javelin can touch it. It churns the ocean like a boiling pot. It leaves a trail of white foam behind it. Nothing on earth is its equal, a creature without fear.

What *are* these creatures? They're not just a hippopotamus and a crocodile, despite what some commentaries suggest. No hippo breathes fire. No crocodile is invulnerable to weapons. These are chaos creatures—ancient symbols of the wild, untamable forces in creation that exist outside human control. They represent the non-order in the world, the things that are powerful and dangerous and unpredictable and that only God can manage.

And that's the point. Job can't control Behemoth. He can't put a leash on Leviathan. He can't even get close to them. But

God made them. God watches over them. God holds them in check—not by eliminating them, but by governing a world where they exist alongside everything else.

The world is not a tidy place. It never was. There are forces of disorder and chaos built into the fabric of creation, and God manages all of it—the beauty and the terror, the lambs and the Leviathans—with a wisdom that no human being can second-guess.

WHAT GOD DIDN'T SAY

Before we move on, it's worth noticing what God *didn't* say. He didn't explain Job's suffering. He didn't say, "Here's why I let this happen to you." He didn't mention the accuser. He didn't tell Job about the heavenly wager. He didn't say Job was being punished, or tested, or taught a lesson. He offered no cause and no reason.

He also didn't say the friends were right. Not one word of God's speech supports the retribution principle. Not one question suggests that Job's suffering has anything to do with hidden sin.

What he *did* say is this: the world is governed by my wisdom, and my wisdom is beyond your comprehension. You can't understand how the rain works, let alone how I manage the forces of chaos. Stop trying to decode the system and start trusting the One who built it.

That's not the same as "I'm God and you're not, so shut up." It's far more than that. It's an invitation—fierce and overwhelming, yes, but an invitation nonetheless—to let go of the need to understand and instead rest in the character of the God who holds all things together.

Job wanted an explanation. God gave him something better. He gave him *himself.*

WHAT THIS MEANS FOR US

First, God doesn't always answer our questions, but he always shows up. Job begged for an audience with God, and he got one. But it didn't look anything like what he expected. God didn't sit down for a calm conversation. He arrived in a storm. Sometimes the answer to our most desperate prayers isn't information; it's presence.

Second, the universe is not designed around us. That's not an insult. It's a liberation. If the world were a simple reward-and-punishment machine centered on human behavior, then every time something went wrong, you'd have to search for what *you* did to cause it. But God sends rain on deserts where no human lives. He delights in wild donkeys that serve no human purpose. His creation is bigger than our story. And that means our suffering doesn't have to mean what we fear it means.

Third, trusting God's wisdom is different from understanding God's plan. Job never got an explanation. He got something more foundational: a reason to trust the One who doesn't owe him an explanation. You don't have to understand the blueprint to trust the architect, especially when the architect shows you enough of the building to take your breath away.

Fourth, the existence of chaos and disorder in the world doesn't mean God has lost control. Behemoth and Leviathan exist. Suffering exists. Unfairness exists. God hasn't eliminated these things, but he hasn't been defeated by them either. He governs a world where order and disorder coexist, and he does it with a wisdom we can glimpse but never master.

TALKING POINTS

1. **God's first words to Job were a rebuke: "Who is this that darkens my counsel?"** Were you surprised that God didn't comfort Job first? Why do you think God started that way?

2. **God asked Job dozens of questions about creation: the stars, the rain, the animals.** None of them had anything to do with Job's suffering. Why do you think God chose to talk about nature instead of answering Job's actual complaint?

3. **God pointed out that he sends rain on deserts where no one lives.** What does that tell us about whether the world revolves around human beings and human purposes?

4. **God asked, "Would you condemn me to justify yourself?"** Have you ever been so sure you were right about something that you were willing to say someone else (maybe even God) was wrong? What's the danger in that?

5. **God described Behemoth and Leviathan as creatures no human can control.** If these represent the wild, chaotic forces in the world, what does it mean that God can manage them but we can't? How does that change the way you think about the things in life that feel out of control?

God has spoken. The whirlwind has roared. The questions have come like waves crashing on a shore. And Job—the man who demanded answers, who signed his name, who dared God to respond—is about to say his final words.

Turn the page.

10

THE END OF THE STORY

Have you ever come out the other side of something you weren't sure you'd survive? Maybe it was a school year that nearly broke you—months of loneliness, or a class that felt impossible, or a friendship that fell apart in slow motion. Maybe it was something at home that shook the ground under your feet and made you wonder if normal would ever come back.

And then one day, almost without you noticing, it was over. Not perfect. Not like it was before. But *over*. You were still standing. You were different now—quieter in some ways, stronger in others—and the world looked both more fragile and more beautiful than it had before.

That's where Job is in chapter 42. The whirlwind has spoken. The questions have rolled like thunder. And now, in the silence that follows the storm, something shifts inside the man who has been fighting for thirty-nine chapters straight.

Job opens his mouth one last time. And what comes out is not a complaint, not a legal argument, not a demand for answers. It's surrender. The real kind, born not from defeat but from seeing clearly for the first time.

"NOW MY EYES HAVE SEEN YOU"

Job's final words to God are brief. After everything—the losses, the debates, the accusations, the oath of innocence, the whirlwind—he says this: "I know that you can do all things; no purpose of yours can be thwarted. You asked, 'Who is this that obscures my plans without knowledge?' Surely I spoke of things I did not understand, things too wonderful for me to know. My ears had heard of you. But now my eyes have seen you. Therefore I take back what I said, and I am done with my dust and ashes."

Read that second-to-last line again. "My ears had heard of you. But now my eyes have seen you."

This is the hinge on which the entire book turns. Before the whirlwind, Job knew *about* God. He knew the theology. He knew the traditions. He could recite what the wise men taught. He had heard the secondhand reports. But all of that knowledge, as real as it was, turned out to be like reading about the ocean versus standing on the shore and watching the waves crash in.

Now Job has *seen* God. Not with his physical eyes. The text isn't describing a literal vision. It's describing the difference between knowing information about someone and actually encountering them. Job's relationship with God has moved from his ears to his eyes, from hearsay to experience, from theology to encounter.

And in the light of that encounter, Job doesn't need the answers he was demanding. He doesn't need the courtroom hearing. He doesn't need the indictment read aloud or the verdict pronounced. The presence of God has replaced the need for an explanation from God.

Job takes back his words. Not his claim of innocence; that was never wrong. What he takes back is his demand that God explain himself, his insistence that he could decode the system, his willingness to put God in the wrong in order to prove himself right. He lets go of his ashes. The mourning is over. Not because the pain wasn't real, but because he's found something bigger than the pain.

THE VERDICT NOBODY EXPECTED

Then God turns to the friends. And what he says stuns everyone. "My anger burns against you and your two friends, because you have not spoken of me what is right, as my servant Job has."

Wait. God is angry at the *friends*? The ones who spent the entire book defending God's justice? The ones who insisted that the universe runs on fair rules and that God always does the right thing? And God approves of *Job*, the one who accused God of injustice, who demanded a courtroom hearing, who said God was his enemy?

This is one of the most shocking reversals in the Bible. But it makes sense when you understand what God values. The friends defended a *system*. Job pursued a *relationship*. The friends explained God with tidy formulas. Job screamed at God with raw honesty. The friends were polite and wrong. Job was outrageous and, in the way that mattered most, right.

God doesn't approve of everything Job said. The whirlwind speeches made that clear. But God would rather have a servant who fights with him than one who defends a cardboard version of him. Job's raging, anguished, relentless pursuit of the real God was closer to the truth than the friends' smooth, confident defense of a God who fits in a box.

God calls Job "my servant" four times in these verses, the same title he gave him at the very beginning, before any of this started. Job's status hasn't changed. His relationship with God is fully intact. The man who was declared blameless in chapter 1 is still blameless in chapter 42. Everything in between was real—the suffering, the anger, the questions, the near-despair—but none of it broke the bond.

Then comes a beautiful detail. God tells the friends to go to Job, offer sacrifices, and have *Job* pray for them. The man they spent three rounds accusing of hidden sin is now their intercessor before God. The man they called a sinner is the one whose prayer God will accept on their behalf.

And Job does it. Without bitterness, without gloating, without conditions. He prays for the friends who wounded him. That act—quiet, generous, unforced—may be the clearest evidence in the entire book that Job truly does serve God for nothing. He's not praying to earn a reward. He's not praying because he has to. He's praying because the encounter with God has changed him, and the man who walks out of the whirlwind is not the same man who walked in.

RESTORATION

Then God restores Job. Double everything. Fourteen thousand sheep instead of seven thousand. Six thousand camels instead of three thousand. A thousand yoke of oxen instead of five hundred. A thousand donkeys instead of five hundred. Seven sons and three daughters. The same number as before, because children aren't possessions to be doubled.

Job's brothers and sisters and old friends come back. They eat together, comfort him, and each one gives him a gift of money and gold. The community that vanished during his suffering reappears now that the storm has passed. It's a realistic detail. People often show up after the worst is over. But it also shows that restoration includes reconciliation with the people around you, not just blessings from above.

Job's three new daughters are named Jemimah, Keziah, and Keren-Happuch, names that speak of beauty and delight. They are described as the most beautiful women in the land, and Job gives them an inheritance alongside their brothers, an act of remarkable generosity and fairness for his time.

Job lives another 140 years. He sees his children and his children's children, four generations deep. And then he dies "old and full of days," the same epitaph given to Abraham, Isaac, and David. The greatest of all the people of the East dies as one of the greatest servants of God who ever lived.

BUT DOES THE ENDING UNDO THE BOOK?

Here's the question you might be asking: doesn't the happy ending contradict everything the book just taught us? If the whole point was that the retribution principle doesn't work, that good behavior doesn't guarantee good outcomes, then why does Job end up with double everything?

The answer matters. Job's restoration is not a reward for passing the test. It's not God saying, "You suffered well, so here's your prize." Job repented with no promise of restoration.

He prayed for his friends with no guarantee that anything would change. He surrendered to God without conditions.

The restoration is grace. It's a gift, freely given, not earned. It reflects who God is: a God who delights in blessing his people, —not a transaction that proves the friends were right after all. The book has spent forty-one chapters demolishing the idea that the world runs on a neat reward-and-punishment system. It would be a terrible misreading to let the last chapter rebuild it.

The restoration also carries a quieter message: God is not a God who takes pleasure in the suffering of those who serve him. The book needed to end with blessing, not because suffering always ends in blessing (it doesn't), but because the God of this story is, at his core, a giver of life. The restoration isn't a guarantee. It's a portrait of God's character.

WHERE JESUS ENTERS

The book of Job never mentions Jesus by name. But it points to him in ways that grow clearer the further you stand from the text.

Job longed for a mediator, someone to stand between him and God. Jesus is that mediator. Job reached for a redeemer, a kinsman who would vindicate him. Jesus is that redeemer. Job discovered that the world runs not on justice but on wisdom, and the New Testament tells us that Jesus *is* the wisdom of God, the one in whom "all the treasures of wisdom and knowledge" are hidden.

And the question that started the whole book, "Does Job fear God for nothing?", finds its ultimate answer not in Job, but in Jesus. Jesus served God with perfect faithfulness. He suffered not for his own sins, but for ours. He was stripped of everything—honor, comfort, friendship, even the sense of his Father's presence—and he did not turn away. He feared God for nothing. He loved to the end.

Job's story whispers what Jesus' story shouts: that trusting God is not about getting something out of it. It's about knowing that God is worthy. Worthy of our trust even when we can't see what he's doing. Worthy of our love even when life is at its darkest. Worthy of our worship even when the only honest prayer we can manage is "I don't understand."

The book is finished. The whirlwind has passed. The ashes are behind you.

But the question the book asked is still alive. And it's not a question about Job anymore. It's a question about you. Do you serve God for nothing? Would you trust him if you lost everything? Would you keep walking toward him even if he never explained why the road was so hard?

You don't have to answer that today. But the book of Job wants you to think about it—carefully, honestly, with your whole heart. Because someday, in some form, the storm will come. And when it does, you'll need more than a formula. You'll need more than a theory. You'll need a God you've actually seen, not just heard about.

Job found that God in the whirlwind.

May you find him too.

INTRODUCTION

Sooner or later, life stops making sense.

Maybe it hasn't happened to you yet. Maybe your world still mostly adds up: you do the right things, things go mostly right, and the people you trust are still trustworthy. But at some point—maybe next year, maybe in ten years, maybe tomorrow—something will happen that doesn't fit the equation. Someone good will get sick. Something unfair will happen to someone who didn't deserve it. You'll watch a person who plays by the rules get crushed while someone who cheats walks away laughing. And a question will rise in your chest that you didn't expect and can't push down: *Why?*

Why do good people suffer? Why does God let terrible things happen to people who love him? Is God even paying attention? And if he is—if he sees everything and has the power to stop it—what does it say about him that he doesn't?

Those aren't new questions. People have been asking them for thousands of years. And there is a book in the Bible that wrestles with them more honestly, more painfully, and more brilliantly than anything else ever written.

It's the book of Job. And it's not what you think it is.

WHY JOB IS DIFFERENT

Most books in the Bible tell a story that moves forward. Genesis starts with creation and ends with a family in Egypt. Exodus follows Israel out of slavery. Joshua leads them into the promised land. There's a beginning, a middle, and an end, and the plot moves from one to the next.

Job doesn't work that way. It starts with a story—a short one, just two chapters—and then it stops. For the next thirty-five chapters, almost nothing *happens*. Instead, people talk. They argue. They accuse. They defend. They vent. They philosophize. They go in circles. And then, finally, God speaks, not to explain, but to ask questions of his own.

If you're expecting an action movie, Job will frustrate you. But if you're willing to sit with the argument, to let the tension build, to feel the weight of questions that don't have easy answers, Job will change how you think about God, about suffering, and about what it really means to have faith.

Job is also different because it doesn't fit neatly into the biblical timeline. It doesn't take place during the exodus or the conquest or the monarchy. Job wasn't an Israelite. He lived in a land called Uz, somewhere east of Israel, probably in the time of the patriarchs. There's no mention of the Law of Moses, no temple, no covenant. Job belongs to the Bible's wisdom literature—the same family as Proverbs and Ecclesiastes—which means it's less interested in telling you *what happened* and more interested in asking *what does it mean?*

What it means, as it turns out, is everything.

THE QUESTION THAT DRIVES THE BOOK

Most people think Job is about suffering. It's not—or at least, not in the way you'd expect. The book never answers the question "Why do good people suffer?" If you come to Job looking for that answer, you'll leave disappointed, the same way people have for three thousand years.

The real question is sharper and more personal: *Does anyone serve God for nothing?*

That question gets asked in the very first chapter. An accuser in God's heavenly court looks at Job, the most righteous man alive, and says, "Of course he worships you. Look at everything you've given him. Take it all away, and he'll curse you to your face."

It's a devastating challenge. Not against Job, but against God. The accuser is saying that God's own system is rigged, that if you reward people for being good, you'll never know whether they're good because they love you or because they love the rewards. The entire book exists to answer that question.

And the answer, when it finally comes, doesn't arrive as an explanation. It arrives as a person: the God of the whirlwind, who shows up not to give Job information but to give Job *himself*.

WHAT YOU'RE ABOUT TO READ

Here's a roadmap of where we're headed.

Chapter 1 covers Job 1–2, the setup: Job's extraordinary life, the heavenly challenge, the catastrophic losses, and Job's stunning response.

Chapter 2 covers Job 3, where Job breaks his silence and

curses the day he was born, one of the rawest expressions of grief in all of Scripture.

Chapter 3 covers Job 4–14, the first round of debate. Three friends—Eliphaz, Bildad, and Zophar—take turns telling Job that his suffering must be his fault. Job pushes back hard.

Chapter 4 covers Job 15–21, where the argument gets uglier. The friends stop offering advice and start describing the doom of the wicked, with every image pointed straight at Job. But Job fires back with one of the most famous declarations in the Bible: "I know that my Redeemer lives."

Chapter 5 covers Job 22–27, where the debate collapses. The friends run out of arguments. Bildad barely speaks. Zophar goes silent. Human wisdom has hit a wall.

Chapter 6 covers Job 28, a breathtaking poem about wisdom—where it can be found, what it costs, and why only God possesses it.

Chapter 7 covers Job 29–31, Job's closing monologue. He looks back on his former life, describes his present misery, and delivers a defiant oath of innocence—daring God to respond.

Chapter 8 covers Job 32–37, the speeches of a young man named Elihu who bursts uninvited into the conversation, angry at everyone and convinced he alone has the answer.

Chapter 9 covers Job 38–41, the climax of the entire book. God finally speaks—from a whirlwind—and what he says isn't what anyone expected.

Chapter 10 covers Job 42, the ending: Job's surrender, God's verdict on the friends, and a restoration that raises as many questions as it answers.

BEFORE YOU BEGIN

A few things to keep in mind.

This is a heavy book. Job deals with loss, grief, physical suffering, and the silence of God. It doesn't flinch. If you've ever gone through something painful, parts of this book will feel uncomfortably familiar. That's intentional. The Bible doesn't pretend life is easy, and neither does Job.

The characters are complicated. Job is the hero of the story, but he says some things about God that will make you wince. The friends are wrong about almost everything, but they're not cartoon villains—they start out genuinely trying to help. God's speeches are magnificent but don't include the one thing Job wanted most: an explanation. Nobody in this book is simple.

There are no easy answers. If you're looking for a formula—do these three things and your suffering will make sense—you won't find one. What you *will* find is something better: a vision of God that is big enough to hold your questions without being threatened by them. Job teaches us that faith isn't the absence of doubt. It's the decision to trust God even when you don't understand what he's doing.

This points to Jesus. The book of Job was written centuries before Jesus was born, but it reaches for him on nearly every page. Job longed for a mediator between himself and God, and Jesus is that mediator. Job cried out for a redeemer, and Jesus is that redeemer. The wisdom poem in chapter 28 says true wisdom belongs to God alone—and the New Testament tells us that Jesus *is* the wisdom of God. The accuser asked whether anyone would serve God for nothing, and Jesus answered that question on the cross, loving God to the uttermost with nothing to gain and everything to lose.

LET'S BEGIN

So here we are, about to open one of the oldest and most important books ever written. We're going to meet a man who had everything and lost it in a single day. We're going to listen to friends who meant well and made everything worse. We're going to hear a young man who thought he had all the answers and an old man who thought he deserved one. And we're going to stand at the edge of a whirlwind and hear the voice of God ask questions that will rearrange the furniture in your mind.

Job won't give you a neat explanation for suffering. But it will give you something more valuable: a God who is big enough to be trusted when life stops making sense.

And if you're anything like me, that's exactly what you need.

Ready? Let's go to the land of Uz.

Turn the page.

1

THE TEST NOBODY SAW

Have you ever done something genuinely kind for someone—not because you had to, not because anyone was watching, but just because you wanted to—and then had somebody say, "You're only being nice because you want something"?

Maybe you helped a friend study for a test, and another kid said, "You're just doing that so she'll let you copy her homework." Maybe you sat with someone at lunch who was alone, and somebody whispered, "You're just trying to look good." Maybe you cleaned the kitchen without being asked, and your sibling said, "You're only doing that because you want something from Mom."

It stings. It stings because they've taken something real—your actual kindness, your actual choice to do the right thing—and turned it into something selfish. They've looked at your heart and decided that the real you is worse than the visible you. That underneath the good behavior, you're just out for yourself.

Now imagine God saying you're the best person alive. Imagine him being proud of you—genuinely, publicly proud. And then imagine someone stepping forward and saying, "The only reason he's good is because you pay him to be. Take away the paycheck and watch what happens."

That's how the book of Job begins. And the question that gets asked in the opening pages is one of the most unsettling questions in the entire Bible: Does anybody serve God for nothing?

THE MAN FROM UZ

The book opens with a quick portrait of a man named Job, and the portrait is almost too good to believe. Job lived in a region called Uz, somewhere east of Israel, probably near the land of Edom. He wasn't an Israelite. He didn't have the Law of Moses or the temple or the covenant. But he knew God, and he lived like it.

The text describes him with four qualities stacked on top of each other like building blocks: he was blameless, upright, feared God, and turned away from evil. That doesn't mean Job was perfect; no one is. It means he was a man of complete integrity. He dealt honestly with people. He took God seriously. When faced with a choice between right and wrong, he consistently chose right.

And God had blessed him for it. Job had seven sons and three daughters, an ideal family by ancient standards. He owned seven thousand sheep, three thousand camels, five hundred yoke of oxen, and five hundred donkeys. He had a massive workforce. The text sums it all up with a single sentence: "This man was the greatest of all the people of the East." If you were making a list of the most successful, most respected, most blessed people in the ancient world, Job would be at the top.

But here's what made Job truly remarkable. It wasn't his

wealth or his family. It was what he did after his kids threw parties. Whenever his sons and daughters held one of their regular feasts, Job would get up early the next morning and offer sacrifices on their behalf just in case one of them had said or thought something dishonoring to God during the celebration. The text says he did this every single time. That's not the behavior of a man going through the motions. That's a man who cared deeply about his relationship with God and wanted his whole family to be right with him.

Everything about Job's life was thriving. His character was impeccable. His family was healthy. His wealth was staggering. His reputation was spotless.

And then the scene shifts to a place Job couldn't see.

BEHIND THE CURTAIN

The story suddenly moves from earth to heaven. The "sons of God," angelic beings who serve in God's council, come to present themselves before the Lord. And among them is a figure the text calls "the accuser."

This figure isn't exactly what most people picture when they hear the word "Satan." The title here literally means "the one who accuses" or "the one who opposes." He's a member of the heavenly court, something like a prosecuting attorney whose job is to ask hard questions and challenge assumptions. He's been roaming the earth, observing, taking notes.

God brings up Job. And he doesn't just mention him casually; he brags about him. "Have you considered my servant Job? There is no one like him on the earth, a blameless and upright man who fears God and turns away from evil."

That's God himself saying Job is the real deal. The finest human being on the planet. Case closed, right?

Not quite. The accuser fires back with a question that cuts to the bone: "Does Job fear God for nothing?"

Think about what he's really asking. He's not saying Job is secretly wicked. He's not denying that Job does all the right things. He's questioning *why* Job does them. His argument goes like this: "Of course Job worships you. Look at everything you've given him! You've built a hedge of protection around him, his family, and everything he owns. His flocks keep multiplying. His life is perfect. Take all that away, and he'll curse you to your face."

The accuser is essentially saying that Job's faith is a transaction. A deal. Job gives God obedience; God gives Job prosperity. Remove the prosperity, and the obedience disappears. Nobody serves God for free.

And here's the part that unsettles people: God accepts the challenge. He gives the accuser permission to strike everything Job has: his possessions, his livestock, even his children. The only restriction is that the accuser can't touch Job himself.

THE WORST DAY IN HISTORY

What happens next is one of the most devastating sequences in all of Scripture. Job is at home. A messenger comes running: the Sabeans (a raiding tribe) attacked and stole all his oxen and donkeys, and killed the servants watching them. "I alone have escaped to tell you."

While that messenger is still talking, another one arrives: fire fell from the sky and burned up all his sheep and the servants tending them. "I alone have escaped to tell you."

While *that* messenger is still speaking, a third bursts in: the Chaldeans formed three raiding parties, swept down on his camels, took them all, and killed the servants. "I alone have escaped to tell you."

And while that messenger is still getting the words out, a fourth arrives with the worst news of all: Job's sons and daughters were eating together at the oldest brother's house when a mighty wind struck the building from every direction. The house collapsed. All ten of them are dead. "I alone have escaped to tell you."

Did you catch the phrase "while he was still speaking"? The disasters didn't come one at a time with days or weeks in between. They came in a single, relentless avalanche. Before Job could process one loss, the next one hit. And the next. And the next. By the time the last messenger finished, Job had lost everything: his wealth, his workers, and all ten of his children.

Job stood up. He tore his robe. He shaved his head—both of these were the customary expressions of grief in his culture. Then he fell to the ground.

And he worshiped.

"Naked I came from my mother's womb, and naked I shall return. The LORD gave and the LORD has taken away. Blessed be the name of the LORD."

The narrator then makes a statement that matters enormously: "In all this, Job did not sin, and he did not blame God for doing anything wrong."

The accuser lost round one.

ROUND TWO

But the accuser wasn't done. Another day arrives, and the heavenly council assembles again. God points to Job a second time, and this time, he adds something: "He still holds fast his integrity, although you moved me against him to ruin him without cause."

Did you catch that? God himself says Job's suffering was "without cause." There was no secret sin. No hidden failure. Job was targeted not because he was guilty, but because he was faithful.

The accuser pushes further. "Skin for skin! A man will give everything he has to save his own life. Strike his body, and he'll curse you to your face." His argument is brutal in its cynicism: people only care about themselves. Take away a man's health, and you'll see who he really is.

God gives permission again, but with one boundary. The accuser can do whatever he wants to Job's body. He just can't kill him.

What follows is horrific. Painful sores erupt all over Job's body, from the soles of his feet to the top of his head. The disease is so severe that Job takes a piece of broken pottery and scrapes his own skin, trying to find some relief from the itching and the pain. He ends up sitting in the ashes outside the city—the place where garbage was burned and outcasts gathered. The wealthiest, most respected man in the East is now unrecognizable, sitting in a garbage heap, scraping his sores with broken dishes.

His wife has been watching all of this. She has lost the same ten children. She has watched her husband's empire crumble and his body fall apart. She comes to him and says, "Are you still holding on to your integrity? Curse God and die."

Before we judge her too harshly, we should try to understand her. This woman buried ten children. She went from being married to the greatest man in the East to watching her husband rot on an ash heap. She wasn't being cruel. She was broken. She had reached the absolute end of herself, and she couldn't bear to watch him suffer anymore.

Job's response is gentle but firm: "Should we accept good from God and not also accept trouble?" And the narrator tells us again: "In all this, Job did not sin with his lips."

SEVEN DAYS OF SILENCE

Word reaches three of Job's friends: Eliphaz, Bildad, and Zophar. They come from different regions, but they share a common purpose: to mourn with Job and comfort him. When they arrive and see him from a distance, they don't recognize him. The disease has so disfigured him that the man they knew is gone. They weep. They tear their own robes. They sprinkle dust on their heads.

And then they do something extraordinary. They sit down on the ground beside him and don't say a word for seven days and seven nights. Seven days. No lectures. No explanations. No attempts to fix him. Just silent presence in the ashes. It's the best thing they do in the entire book.

Unfortunately, they won't stay silent. But for now, in this moment, they are exactly the friends Job needs—people who show up, who sit in the wreckage, and who don't try to explain it away.

WHAT THIS MEANS FOR US

First, the most important question in this book is not "Why do people suffer?" It's "Does anyone serve God for nothing?" The accuser's challenge forces us to look at our own motives. Do you follow God because of what you get out of it: comfort, blessing, answers to prayer, the promise of heaven? Or would you follow him even if all of that disappeared? That's an uncomfortable question, but it's the question the entire book of Job is built on.

Second, sometimes the worst things happen to the best people. And there is no hidden reason. God himself called Job's suffering "without cause." There was no secret sin, no lesson Job needed to learn, no divine punishment being handed down. Sometimes suffering just doesn't have a tidy explanation. The book of Job is honest about that from the very first pages.

Third, grief is not the opposite of faith. Job tore his robe, shaved his head, fell to the ground, and then he worshiped. He didn't pretend the pain wasn't real. He didn't paste on a smile and say everything was fine. He grieved deeply and he worshiped honestly, and the text says both of those things happened at the same time without contradiction. You don't have to choose between hurting and believing.

Fourth, the best thing a friend can do for someone who is suffering is simply show up. Eliphaz, Bildad, and Zophar got it exactly right for seven days. They came. They sat. They wept. They said nothing. No advice. No theology lessons. No explanations. Just presence. When someone you love is going through something terrible, your presence matters more than your words.

TALKING POINTS

1. **The accuser claimed that Job only served God because of what he got out of it.** Be honest—do you think most people follow God for what they'll receive in return? What would it look like to serve God "for nothing"?

2. **Job's wife told him to curse God and die.** Why do you think she said that? What does her response tell us about how suffering affects not just the person going through it, but the people around them?

3. **When the four messengers brought their news, each one arrived "while he was still speaking."** Why do you think the author described the disasters this way? What does the pacing tell us about what Job experienced?

4. **Job worshiped God right after losing everything.** Does that seem natural to you, or does it feel forced? How do you think you would respond if something devastating happened to you?

5. **The three friends sat in silence for seven days.** Why do you think that was the right thing to do? When someone is hurting, why is it so hard for us to just be quiet and be present instead of trying to say the right thing?

Job has passed the test, twice. But the silence is about to break. The friends are going to open their mouths, and when they do, everything changes. Job's real struggle is just beginning.

Turn the page.

2

THE DAY THE DAM BROKE

Have you ever held it together—really held it together—through something awful, and then completely fallen apart later when nobody expected it?

Maybe your dog died, or your parents told you they were getting divorced, or you got cut from the team. And at first you were fine. You kept going. You went to school. You answered people's questions. You told everyone you were okay. Maybe you even believed it for a while.

Then one night, lying in bed, or sitting in the car, or standing in the shower, something snapped. Everything you'd been holding back came flooding out all at once, and it hit you harder than it had on the day it actually happened. The tears came. The anger came. The thoughts came that you'd been pushing down for days or weeks. And if someone had been standing next to you at that moment, they would have been shocked. They would have thought, "Where did *this* come from?"

It came from the dam breaking.

That's what happens in Job 3. For seven days, Job has been sitting in ashes with his three friends in total silence. He's lost everything: his children, his wealth, his health. He's covered in sores, scraping his skin with broken pottery, barely recognizable. And for a full week, he hasn't said a word.

Then he opens his mouth. And what comes out is not what anyone expected.

Job doesn't ask a question. He doesn't blame anyone. He doesn't launch into a theological argument. Instead, he curses the day he was born. "Let the day I was born disappear. Let the night someone said, 'A boy has been conceived,' be wiped from existence."

That's how it starts. And it only gets more intense from there. Job wants the day of his birth erased from the calendar—swallowed by darkness, blotted out as if it never happened. He uses the language of creation in reverse. In Genesis 1, God said, "Let there be light," and light pierced the darkness. Job says the opposite: let that day be darkness. Let no light shine on it. Let thick clouds cover it. Let it be as if God never called that day into being.

Then he moves further back, to the night he was conceived. He wants that night removed from the number of months. He wants it to be barren, empty, as though it never produced anything at all. No joyful cry. No dawn the next morning. Nothing.

Job is doing something extraordinary here. He's not just saying, "I wish I were dead." He's saying, "I wish I had never existed." He wants to undo his own creation. He wants to reverse the moment when God first gave him life.